P9-CLV-019

TWENTIETH CENTURY VIEWS

The aim of this series is to present the best in contemporary critical opinion on major authors, providing a twentieth century perspective on their changing status in an era of profound revaluation.

Maynard Mack, *Series Editor*
Yale University

ARTHUR MILLER

A COLLECTION OF CRITICAL ESSAYS

Edited by

Robert W. Corrigan

Prentice-Hall, Inc.   A SPECTRUM BOOK   *Englewood Cliffs, N. J.*

Acknowledgments

I want to thank Grace Schulman, Dianne Young, Cathy Hill, and especially Ellen Brooks, to whom this book is dedicated, for all of their help. Without it, I would never have completed the book.

R.W.C.

Contents

ARTHUR MILLER

Introduction:
The Achievement of Arthur Miller

by Robert W. Corrigan

I

We live in an instant age. Everything from the most complex informa-
tion to giant buildings, from vast networks of electric circuitry to blender-
ized gourmet meals, can be produced or made available in a flash. It
should be of little wonder, then, that we also tend to create instant major
figures in the arts; and our theatre has been no exception. Of the five
most important Americans writing for the theatre in the twentieth century—Eugene O'Neill, Thornton Wilder, Tennessee Williams, Arthur
Miller, and Edward Albee—only O'Neill's reputation and stature were
built cumulatively over a long period of time. And of the five, only
O'Neill (and possibly Williams) approached the level of productivity
achieved by their continental counterparts. Each of the other four was
granted the status of "major" playwright with the professional production of his first or second full-length play (Wilder: *Our Town,* first, 1938;
Williams: *The Glass Menagerie,* second, 1945; Miller: *All My Sons,* second, 1947; Albee: *Who's Afraid of Virginia Woolf?,* first, 1962). An international reputation can be a heavy burden for an artist to bear at any
time, but it is particularly difficult when thrust upon him early in his
career.

This was definitely true for Arthur Miller. After *Death of a Salesman*
was produced in 1949, he was considered by many as one of the world's
most important living dramatists, and he was treated as a monument
while still very much alive. Fortunately, Miller knew how to cope with
such adulation and was not destroyed by it. But such conditions did
create an atmosphere which has made it difficult to consider his artistic

achievement with objectivity. Now that more than twenty years have elapsed since he was first catapulted to fame, it is possible for us to see the pattern of his work a little more clearly.

Although one should be wary of critics who play the "periods game" and break down an artist's work into nice, tight little compartments, there do, nonetheless, seem to be two quite different patterns of concern in the plays that Arthur Miller has written thus far. The first pattern emerges in the plays written up to, and including, the revised version of *A View from the Bridge* (1957). The second began to emerge in *The Misfits* (1960), Miller's only produced film, and has become increasingly manifest in his last three plays, *After the Fall, Incident at Vichy,* and *The Price.* I believe these patterns can be best discussed by treating them as separate yet related aspects of the playwright's evolution as an artist.

In tracing this development, Erik Erikson's remarkable psychological biography, *Young Man Luther,* can be especially helpful. In this book, Dr. Erikson postulates the idea that in the lives of most people there are normally three periods of psychological crisis: the crisis of Identity, the crisis of Generativity, and the crisis of Integrity. These crises, he maintains, generally occur in youth, middle age, and old age, respectively, although there is always some overlapping and the pattern does vary slightly from individual to individual.

I believe that the first two stages in Erikson's pattern of psychological crisis are quite applicable to Miller's development as a playwright and that they throw light on the major themes of everything he has thus far written. The central conflict in all of the plays in Miller's first period (*The Man Who Had All the Luck*—1944, *All My Sons*—1947, *Death of a Salesman*—1949, *An Enemy of the People*—1950, *The Crucible*—1953, *A Memory of Two Mondays*—1955, *A View from the Bridge*—1955, *A View from the Bridge*—1957) grows out of a crisis of identity. Each of the protagonists in these plays is suddenly confronted with a situation which he is incapable of meeting and which eventually puts his "name" in jeopardy. In the ensuing struggle it becomes clear that he does not know what his name really is; finally, his inability to answer the question "Who am I?" produces calamity and his ultimate downfall. Strange as it may sound, Joe Keller, Willy Loman, John Proctor, and Eddie Carbone are alike, caught up in a problem of identity that is normally characteristic of youth (one is almost tempted to say adolescence), and their deaths are caused by their lack of self-understanding. In every case this blindness is in large measure due to their failure to have resolved the question of identity at an earlier and more appropriate time in life. Miller presents this crisis as a conflict between the uncomprehending self and a solid social or economic structure—the family, the community, the system. The drama emerges either when the protagonist breaks his connection with society or when unexpected pressures reveal that such a connection has in fact never even existed. Miller sees the need for such a connection as absolute, and the failure to achieve and/or maintain it is bound to result in catastrophe. He makes this very clear in his introduction to *The Collected Plays,* where he writes about *All My Sons* as follows:

> Joe Keller's trouble, in a word, is not that he cannot tell right from wrong, but that his cast of mind cannot admit that he, personally, has any viable connection with his world, his universe, or his society.[1]

Miller expands this idea even further in an article in *The New York Times* written on the occasion of the New York revival of *A View from the Bridge*:

> What kills Eddie Carbone is nothing visible or heard, but the built-in conscience of the community whose existence he has menaced by betraying it. Whatever both plays [the other was *A Memory of Two Mondays*] are, they are at bottom reassertions of the existence of community.[2]

Each of the plays written prior to *The Misfits* is a judgment of a man's failure to maintain a viable connection with his surrounding world because he does not know himself. The verdict is always guilty, and it is a verdict based upon Miller's belief that if each man faced up to the truth about himself, he could be fulfilled as an individual and still live within the restrictions of society. But while Miller's judgments are absolute, they are also exceedingly complex. There is no doubt that he finally stands four-square on the side of the community, but until the moment when justice must be served, his sympathies are for the most part directed toward those ordinary little men who never discovered who they really were.

A Miller protagonist belongs to a strange breed. In every instance he is unimaginative, inarticulate (as with Buechner's Woyzeck, the words that would save him seem always to be just beyond his grasp) and

---

[1] *The Collected Plays,* p. 19.
[2] *The New York Times,* Sunday, August 15, 1965.

physically nondescript, if not downright unattractive.[3] His roles as husband and father (or father-surrogate) are of paramount importance to him, and yet he fails miserably in both. He wants to love and be loved, but he is incapable of either giving or receiving love. And he is haunted by aspirations toward a joy in life that his humdrum spirit is quite unable to realize. Yet, in spite of all these negative characteristics, Miller's protagonists do engage our imagination and win our sympathies. I think this ambiguity stems from the fact that his own attitude towards his creations is so contradictory.

On the one hand, he finds them guilty for their failure to maintain (or fulfill) their role within the established social structure; though there is something almost rabbinical in the loving sternness of his judgments.[4] On the other hand, while it is certainly true that the system is ultimately affirmed, it cannot be denied that the system is shown to be in some ways responsible for creating those very conditions which provoke the protagonists' downfall.

Despite these contradictions, each of the plays of Miller's first period is imbued with a sure sense of the world. The individual may struggle for his name, to be himself in difficult situations in what may seem to be an inimical world, but a sense of what Miller believes the world can and should be is always there. The issues facing each of the protagonists are clearcut, and we cannot help feeling that if they had chosen otherwise (such an alternative is open to them) the conflict would have dissolved. Unlike the most significant tragedies of the past—and Miller certainly had conscious aspirations to be a tragic writer during this period of his career—the catastrophes in these plays do not have a sense of inevitability, nor do they spring from the unalterable divisions of man's nature. The world of Arthur Miller's first plays is a hermetic one; one in which none of life's mysteries have been allowed to intrude. The reader

---

[3] Henry Popkin, in an article which regrettably could not be included in this volume, underscores this fact when he points out that all the leading actors in the major productions of Miller's plays have been rough-hewn types: Lee Cobb, Thomas Mitchell, Ed Begley, Raf Vallone, Van Heflin, Arthur Kennedy, J. Carroll Naish, Jason Robards, and Pat Hingle.

[4] A number of critics have made the point that Miller's Jewish heritage is one of the dominant motivating forces in his theatrical mode. I do not quarrel with this view, particularly as it applies to the plays of his first period; they do seem to have several characteristics which we tend to associate with traditional Jewish family life. My own experience and background are such, however, that I do not feel competent to explore this dimension of Miller's work. Moreover, I do not believe the central conflicts of these plays and Miller's attitude toward his protagonists to be uniquely Jewish.

or spectator may be caught up in the suspense of the plot, but he always knows where he is, just as Miller seems to know.[5]

It is this quality of certainty which characterizes *The Collected Plays.* This volume, published in 1957, marks the completion of the first phase of his development, and one senses from the Introduction that Miller was capable of an objective assessment of his own work which only an artist secure in his achievement could succeed in making. Like his protagonists, however, Miller was in for a shock. The closed and tight world of the first plays was soon to be shattered. Unlike his protagonists, he was not destroyed. He emerged from a period of painful personal conflict to write plays with significantly new and wider dimensions.

II

The Collected Plays was dedicated to Miller's second wife, Marilyn Monroe, who was to be the inspiration for his next work, *The Misfits* (1960). Much has been written about this relationship, and while I have no intention of adding to the pile of surmise and irrelevancy, I think it is undeniable that Miller's marriage to Miss Monroe had a profound effect on his attitudes, his sense of the world, his view of himself, and perhaps even on the nature of his dramatic form. These changes first became apparent in *The Misfits,* a screenplay which I consider the pivotal work in Miller's career as a playwright, although it has been unaccountably neglected in most appraisals of his work. One is aware that a transition is taking place, because *The Misfits* is the first of Miller's dramas which is not concerned with identity. Each of the five characters is very much alone, and none of them—like the wild mustangs who symbolize their condition—fits into the world as it exists; but identity is never one of the play's issues.[6]

---

[5] "I was trying in *Salesman,* in this respect, to set forth what happens when a man does not have a grip on the forces of life and has no sense of values which will lead him to that kind of a grip; but the implication was that there must be such a grasp of those forces, or else we're doomed. I was not, in other words, Willy Loman, I was the writer, and Willy Loman is there because I could see beyond him." From "Morality and Modern Drama; Arthur Miller, as interviewed by Phillip Gelb," *The Educational Theatre Journal,* October, 1958, pp. 198–99.

[6] Henceforth I shall usually refer to *The Misfits* as a play even though it is, in Miller's words, "neither novel, play nor screenplay." It is, he goes on, "a story conceived as a film, and every word is there for the purpose of telling the camera what to see and the actors what they are to say."

Gay, the chief protagonist, always knows who he is, and the intrusion of Roslyn into his life does not make him question his identity; rather, her presence comes to make him conscious of an absence, an emptiness, in his existence. Guido is certainly not a character with self-knowledge; in fact, he has numerous blind spots. But his blindness about himself is not central to the action, and the situation never forces him to question his identity. Even the younger Perce, whose age, psychological condition, and family situation are rooted in an identity crisis, does not play this kind of role in the drama. If anything, his very presence points up the fact that this is *not* what the play is about. Roslyn is a much more complex character. While she is "a woman whose life has forbidden her to forsake her loneliness," she also has the childlike innocence and trust of one who exists before the fall. She has no sense of her self at all, or perhaps it is more accurate to say that, like a child, she is an emerging self who has yet to have a consciousness of her own identity. Thus, in a way, all of these are new Miller characters, whose very natures preclude the crisis of identity from becoming a dramatic element.

A still more noticeable change between *The Misfits* and the plays that preceded it is Miller's radically different attitude toward sex and the role of woman. In the plays of the first period, the woman is always in the background. She is never sexually interesting and is always a mother figure even when she is a wife. There is a marked streak of puritanism in Miller's view of women in these plays, a puritanism which is clearly underscored by such lines as "Our opposites are always clothed in sexual sin," or "It's a cold wife that prompts lechery." Quite unlike Tennessee Williams' plays written during the same period, desire is not a central part of Miller's universe, and his plays are manifestly lacking in the sensual.

Yet, if sexuality is submerged in the plays of the first period, it is not dormant; in its repressed state, sex plays an important role in the action. In fact, it is always the cause of catastrophe. Chris and Sue's relationship is the beginning of Joe Keller's undoing in *All My Sons*; Willy's affair in Boston is the cause of his separation from Biff; Proctor's act of adultery with Abby is the source of his downfall; and Carbone's incestuous and unacknowledged passion for Catherine is the cause of his death. In every play the sexual sin brings on disaster. The stability of the family—the value Miller always affirms—is inevitably shattered when sex rears its ugly and sinful head.

One can speculate (and many have) as to whether Miller's marriage to

Miss Monroe (the puritan and the sex goddess) caused a shift in his attitudes. There can be no question that a change did occur. It is first revealed in the actual evolution of *The Misfits*. Originally, this work was written as a short story for *Esquire* in 1957, when Miller was in Reno getting a divorce from his first wife. While in this city of sad, lonely, and oftentimes desperate people, his own solid family world having crumbled, Miller seems to have become aware of separateness and of a kind of people who have no place in a system. It is significant, however, that the short story reveals this misfit condition in terms of a totally masculine world. After his marriage to Miss Monroe, when he comes to redo the story for the film, a woman is added; that woman is his second wife. For the first time, a woman shares the central focus in a Miller work. In fact, the role of Roslyn is so dominant that at times she draws our attention away from Gay altogether.

It is interesting to note that there is no family in *The Misfits*—again, it is the first time—only the tortured comradeship of a group of people who belong nowhere. Like them, Miller seems to be cut off from the structures and strictures of the past, in a world that is lonely and adrift. "To life—whatever that is," Roslyn says, in a toast after her divorce. No character in the earlier plays could have or would have made such a statement. Similarly, Gay's loose-end philosophy of "Just live," because "maybe all there really is is what happens next, just the next thing, and you're not supposed to remember anybody's promises," is a credo totally alien to the clearly defined and highly circumscribed attitudes of the previous plays.

But the aspect of *The Misfits* which I find most significant (and the element which clearly indicates that Miller is moving in a new direction) is the fact that it marks the beginning of what has become his growing involvement with the dramatic possibilities of otherness. The characters in *The Misfits* are not so much concerned with themselves as they are with finding a way to relate to each other. In this struggle, Roslyn is the catalyst. For the most part, the play focuses on separation, but by the end of the film Gay and Roslyn have finally touched. For the first time they are fully aware of their need for each other, and yet in their need neither of them feels compelled to deprive the other of his selfhood. This ending is, at best, tentatively hopeful (not sentimental, as some critics have said). Like the quiet moment between Hannah and Shannon at the end of Williams' *The Night of the Iguana*, it is an intimation of the possible rather than an affirmation of it.

This moment has not been achieved without difficulty, however.[7] At the beginning of the film, both Gay and Roslyn are very much alone. She has just gotten a divorce from a husband who wasn't there ("why can't I just say he wasn't *there?* I mean, you could touch him but he wasn't there.") and he has just put the latest of a long line of divorcees on a train back to St. Louis. But while the external situation is similar, their inner condition is totally different. Roslyn is perpetually alone. She and the world have always been strangers. As a result, she seems never to have been touched by life. Her open innocence is not assumed; rather it is the response of one who has never found a way to live. Gay, on the other hand, knows life all too well and wants no part of it. He is determined to stay free, not just from the world of wages, but from anything that demands a commitment. He says, "I hunt these horses to keep myself free," and while this is true, Miller makes a more telling comment about him when he describes him as follows: "He needs no guile because he has never required himself to promise anything, so his betrayals are minor and do not cling."

To promise is the key to the whole work. Roslyn has never really made any promises because she doesn't know how to, and Gay never has because he has refused to do so. (In renouncing his former wife and children, he broke the only real promise he seems ever to have made.) And yet promises are not only the basis of all enduring and meaningful human relationships; they are also the only things that can give stability to existence. In this regard, Hannah Arendt once wrote:

> The possible redemption from the predicament of irreversibility—of being unable to undo what one has done—is the faculty of forgiving. The remedy for unpredictability, for the chaotic uncertainty of the future, is contained in the faculty to make and keep promises. . . . Both faculties depend upon plurality, on the presence and acting of others, for no man can forgive himself and no man can be bound by a promise made only to himself.[8]

The central action of *The Misfits* is the steady movement of Gay and Roslyn from two extremes of isolation until they can meet and make

---

[7] Though the whole story is under a shadow of foreboding that the relationship between Gay and Roslyn will explode, the tone of the work is never grim, morbid, or heavy. I believe Miller achieves this remarkable balance because the characters—with the possible exception of Guido—never feel sorry for themselves in their misfit and isolated condition.

[8] Hannah Arendt, *The Human Condition* (New York: Doubleday Anchor Book Edition), pp. 212–13.

a promise to each other. And they make this promise with full respect for "the otherness" of the other.[9] The symbol of this promise is their decision to have a child. When Gay first proposes the idea, Roslyn rejects it because the bond-promise still does not exist between them. It is only after the struggle with the mustangs that such a relationship can occur. Roslyn must come to accept what the wild horses mean to Gay no matter how horrifying she finds the experience; and he, in turn, must come to see that true freedom can only be found in relationship, in the acceptance of otherness. His real act of freedom is the releasing of the stallion for Roslyn's sake. Only then does he discover that he has "touched the whole world." Then they can make the deepest of human promises: to have a child.

III

As I said earlier, the Arthur Miller of *The Misfits* is quite different from the author of the works included in *The Collected Plays,* and *The Misfits* marks a new departure not only in form but in tone and theme as well. The stern moralist has softened. For the first time in his career, Miller has not led his characters to the seat of judgment. He accepts, and even loves, these misfit souls; he does not judge them. From this point on, in each of the three plays which have followed *The Misfits,* he has been primarily concerned with the implications of otherness in both the private and the public levels of experience. Such a concern inevitably leads him to come to grips with those conflicts which are inherent in the crisis of generativity.

The identity crisis, which is at the heart of the plays of Miller's first period, is a crisis of consciousness. The generativity crisis is one of con-

---

[9] Although Miller never uses the word, this might be called love. Certainly, it is love in the way defined by Thomas Merton in *Disputed Questions,* where he writes:

to love another as an object is to love him as "a thing," as a commodity which can be used, exploited, enjoyed and then cast off. But to love another as a person we must begin by granting him his own autonomy and identity as a person. We have to love him for his own good, not for the good we get out of him. And this is impossible unless we are capable of a love which "transforms" us, so to speak, into the other person, making us able to see things as he sees them, love what he loves, experience the deeper realities of his own life as if they were our own. Without sacrifice, such a transformation is utterly impossible. But unless we are capable of this kind of transformation "into the other" while remaining ourselves, we are not yet capable of a fully human existence.

science. In such a condition, as Dr. Erikson describes it, the individual must face up to the fact that "I have done this and that; my acts have affected others in this or that way. Have I done well or ill? Can I justify the influence which, intentionally or unintentionally, I have had on others?" This is the essential drama of all Miller's plays beginning with *After the Fall*. It is the drama of someone who knows and accepts his identity and is conscious of his unique relationship to other people. The protagonists of Miller's first period struggled, for the most part unsuccessfully, to discover who they were. In his last three plays, Miller is concerned with the effect his protagonists have had on others and their capacity to accept full responsibility for what they have or have not done.

After the Fall is a dramatic revelation of a man who has come to realize that each one of us has, indeed, been born after the fall of man and that, if we are ever to know ourselves, we must recognize and accept the fact that we not only have a share in the fall, but perpetuate it.[10] All of Miller's heroes have a tremendous sense of guilt. In the earlier plays, however, they could never really acknowledge that the source of guilt was in themselves, because they did not know themselves and therefore could not know their guilt—even though they were destroyed by it. Only when we become aware of other people as separate identities who exist in and for themselves, and not merely as extensions of our own needs and concerns, can we be capable of seeing how our deeds can and do affect them. With such awareness we come to recognize that we are responsible for what happens not only to ourselves, but, insofar as we relate to others, to them as well. This is the condition of Quentin at the opening of *After the Fall*. He is clearly caught up in a generativity crisis. He is painfully aware of the fact that he has acted on others; he is also aware of the people in his life *as* others.

In general, most people think of *After the Fall* as Miller's *mea culpa*. This is to miss the point of the play completely. In spite of all the flashbacks, this is not a memory play, any more than *Death of a Salesman* is one. The motive force of *After the Fall* is Quentin's desire and need to enter into a relationship with Holga. But desiring and needing Holga is no longer a simple thing because Quentin is also aware—and it is a new awareness for a Miller character—that to enter into a relationship

---

[10] In a special Foreword to the play written for its first publication in *The Saturday Evening Post*, Miller underscores this point when he writes: "The human being becomes 'himself' in the act of becoming aware of his sinfulness. He 'is' what he is ashamed of."

with Holga is to be responsible for her and for what happens to her because of what he himself does and has done. (By extension, to relate to one individual is to accept a personal responsibility for what happens to all men. This is the significance of the many flashbacks to the concentration camp, and it is a theme which Miller develops further in *Incident at Vichy*.)[11]

Miller has called *After the Fall* a trial ("the trial of a man by his own conscience, his own values, his own deeds"). In a sense this is true, but it is also misleading. The play is certainly not a trial play in the same way that the earlier plays are, where the judgment is the final verdict and where the laws of life which have been violated are viewed as a taskmaster bringing us back to the paths of righteousness by making us more aware. The play is about commitment and choice. "Can I commit myself again?" is the agonizing question that Quentin asks himself. And to answer that question, he must face the evidence, must face up to the fact that everything that he has ever done *is* the evidence. ("A life, after all, is evidence, and I have two divorces in my safe-deposit box.") But to search for a verdict is not the issue; in fact, it is a cop-out. How can there be a verdict when there is "no judge in sight"? And how purposeful are our own self-judgments? The real challenge facing Quentin is to accept the validity of the evidence without resorting to "the everlasting temptation of innocence." Not to accept is to live a life of "pointless litigation of existence before an empty bench."

The first stage of his acceptance consists of becoming fully conscious of the otherness of all the people who have been a part of his life. (Significantly, as he recalls the past, Quentin is able to think of them as people rather than as extensions of himself. He is able to see his parents and his first wife as they were—at least in some respects—and also as they saw him, even when this was not a pleasant vision.) Such awareness leads him to acceptance of his responsibility for what has happened to

---

[11] Again, Miller makes this point clear in his Foreword: "Quentin . . . arrives on the scene weighed down with a sense of his own pointlessness and the world's. His success as an attorney has crumbled in his hands as he sees only his own egotism in it and no wider goal beyond himself. He has lived through two wrecked marriages. His desperation is too serious, too deadly to permit him to blame others for it. He is desperate for a clear view of his own responsibility for his life, and this because he has recently found a woman he feels he can love, and who loves him; he cannot take another life into his own hands hounded as he is by self-doubt. He is faced, in short, with . . . the terrifying fact of choice. And to choose, one must know oneself, but no man knows himself who cannot face the murder in him, the sly and everlasting complicity with the forces of destruction."

them. He must accept his share of Lou's death, his inadequacy in his relationship with Louise, Maggie's life-blood on his hands. But accepting the evidence involves much more than just acknowledging our role in the big events or the major relationships of our lives; it means facing up to the idea that everything we do affects other people. This is the significance of Felice, who weaves in and out of the play. Even the smallest gesture, which had no significance for Quentin, profoundly shapes her life.[12] That is part of the evidence too.

Quentin's presentation of the evidence (his past life) is not, however, the central point of the play. At the end of the first act, after glancing at Holga, he says: "It's that the evidence is bad for promises. But how do you touch the world without a promise?" Here we are back again with the main theme of *The Misfits*. Only with a promise can we touch the world, and a promise involves both an awareness of "what I had done, what had been done to me, and even what I ought to do" and a responsibility for the otherness of another human being.

After the Fall thus marks a real progression in Miller's attitudes. The question of identity is never an issue. The name theme of the earlier plays does, in fact, re-emerge at the end of the play, and it is important to see that when Maggie challenges him by trying to make him nameless ("You're on the end of a long, long line, Frank!"), Quentin is not destroyed, but able to accept his "own blood-covered name." The play also goes beyond *The Misfits*. Gay and Roslyn had a glimpse of what relationship might be, but they still hadn't made the journey. At the end of the play they were still simply talking about it:

> *Roslyn:* How do you find your way back in the dark?
> *Gay:* Just head for that big star straight on. The highway's under it; take us right home.

The trip "home" isn't easy. To get home you have to face up to your responsibility for others. This is something Gay has never done (having never made promises) nor has Roslyn (who has never been able to transcend her isolation). Quentin, on the other hand, is in the process of the journey—all of the last plays are a part of the journey—the first step of which is to accept the fact that we have affected and continually do affect other people's lives.

---

[12] This prefigures the beginning of his relationship with Maggie. The opening episode with her is equally inconsequential yet consequential. It has disastrous results because a relationship which could never be maintained grows from that encounter.

As Quentin goes to meet Holga, he goes with the knowledge that he is a murderer, that he bears the mark of Cain. He moves toward her with no sense of certainty, but with that kind of courage—probably the only kind there is—which is born of doubt. *After the Fall* significantly ends with a beginning ("Hello"), just as *The Misfits* did. However, now there is a knowing. The big question we are left with at the end of the play is "Is the knowing all?" Miller himself does not seem to know the answer. But in *Incident at Vichy* and *The Price*, he carries the question further.

IV

When compared to *After the Fall, Incident at Vichy* may seem to be a smaller play. In many ways it is, but it does reveal the next stage in Miller's development of his new theme: our personal responsibility for our murderous nature. *After the Fall* ends with Quentin acknowledging that we act as we do because "no man lives who would not rather be the sole survivor of this place than all its finest victims." He knows that he gave all of the people in his life "willingly to failure and to death that I might live." In *Incident at Vichy*, the psychiatrist Leduc knows the same thing and represents a similar attitude. But there are some important differences.

Leduc has an anger which Quentin lacked. He directs this anger at himself (for thinking of using his own death as a way of taking vengeance on a wife he no longer loves), at all men for their failure ever to learn from man's history of slaughter and destruction, and especially at Prince Von Berg, whose special circumstances will save him from the Nazi horror. Moreover, though the anger turns to frustration when he must acknowledge that knowing isn't enough and that he has failed not only to "make part of myself what I know," but to "teach others the truth," he is in fact a better teacher than he realizes. In the climactic speech of the remarkable *agon* which closes the play, he says to Von Berg:

. . . I have never analyzed a gentile who did not have, somewhere hidden in his mind, a dislike if not a hatred for the Jews. . . . Until you know it is true of you, you will destroy whatever truth can come of the atrocity. Part of knowing who we are is knowing we are not someone else. And Jew is only the name we give to that stranger, that agony we cannot feel, that death we look at like a cold abstraction. Each man has his Jew; it is the other. And the

Jews have their Jews. And now, now above all, you must see that you have yours—the man whose death leaves you relieved that you are not him, despite your decency. And that is why there is nothing and will be nothing—until you face your own complicity with this . . . your own humanity.

He concludes the scene by saying: "It's not your guilt I want, it's your responsibility—that might have helped." In many ways this is only an amplification of the basic theme of *After the Fall.* What carries *Incident at Vichy* further is the fact that Von Berg—who has much the same kind of innocence about life as Roslyn and Maggie—is shown to be capable of the pure act of courage. He gives up his freedom (and presumably his life) for another. To have such courage is to transcend the human. And yet it is precisely this kind of superhuman capacity that all of the most significant dramas in the theatre's history have celebrated as the source of man's greatness.

The major theme of *Incident at Vichy* is that responsibility is not just a question of personal relationships; it must also extend to the world. Here Miller broadens the focus of his theme. What was implied by the projection of the concentration camp in *After the Fall* becomes the subject of *Incident at Vichy.* The most interesting (and I think perhaps the most significant) realization of the theme emerges at the very last moment. When Von Berg comes out of the Nazi office, having been cleared, he gives his pass (the means to freedom) to Leduc. The doctor not only does not want to take it, but is almost horrified at the thought of it. His final speech, together with Miller's stage direction, reads as follows:

> *Leduc backs away, his hands springing to cover his eyes in the awareness of his own guilt.*
> *Leduc—a plea in his voice:* I wasn't asking you to do this! You don't owe me this!

The real mark of Cain—and the reason why there will always be a Melos, a Vichy, a Memphis—is that the murderer within us cannot stand the thought that someone else could and would give up his life for our sake. Such an act makes our guilt unbearable by destroying that balance of *quid pro quo* which we have created in an effort to justify our guilt. We suppose that the price life exacts for our existence should be fair, and the actions of a Von Berg or a Martin Luther King upset the balance of payments. We cannot permit ourselves to be in someone else's debt.

There must always be a price. That is why there must also always be a Jew.

It is this concern with life's balance of payments that Miller explores in his most recent play, *The Price*. At the end of *After the Fall*, as Quentin goes to join Holga, he asks himself, "Is the knowing all?" Is the hard-won awareness enough? Can such knowledge be the basis of a commitment to another human being? *Incident at Vichy* answers these questions, and the answer is "No! It is not enough." We must also, as Leduc puts it, "make part of myself what I know," and we must make others come to see this truth. The great insight of *Incident at Vichy* is that we fail in this because of our inability to accept the otherness of people and, more important, because our guilt-ridden natures will not permit anyone to acknowledge our own otherness. Locked in the prison of self, our guilt demands that there be a price—no free giving like Von Berg's—because then solipsism becomes intolerable. It is this solipsism which makes us incapable of love, which makes us treat others and our relationships with them as commodities, as objects which, to use Merton's words again, "can be used, exploited, enjoyed and then cast off." This guilt is first revealed in our insistence that "vengeance be mine." Leduc sees this attitude in his relationship with his wife and can acknowledge it to Von Berg because he still believes in his moral superiority over the Prince. But when Von Berg freely offers his own life to save the Jewish doctor, Leduc's essential guilt—of which his vengeance is symptomatic —is fully expressed. The ending of *Incident at Vichy* reveals that otherness is an ambiguous reality. Without it there can be no promises. and hence no love; but, at the same time, its very existence calls forth the murder which each of us carries within himself.

In *The Price*, Miller develops these themes further. This play, while longer than *Incident at Vichy*, is written with the same tight and simple form, and in it he returns to the family as the locus of the action.[13] The play consists essentially of the confrontation of two brothers who have been estranged for sixteen years. Each of them has reacted in different

---

[13] The family seems to provide the most hospitable context for Miller's theatre. He certainly is both more at ease and more direct when he writes out of and in terms of familial conflicts. If one can fault *Incident at Vichy* in any way, it would have to be because of its tendency to abstractness. Most of the characters represent attitudes and lack the sense of a felt life. Whatever passion they have tends, for the most part, to be rhetorical rather than an inherent quality of character. This is certainly not the case with Victor and Walter in *The Price*.

ways to the terror provoked by their father's failure in the Depression
and has now returned to the old family brownstone to sell the parents'
possessions before the building is demolished. Victor, a policeman with
twenty-eight years on the force, has chosen the security of a humdrum
but safe existence, justifying his (and his wife's) sense of failure on the
grounds that he has sacrificed his own ambitions to take care of his
broken father. Walter, on the other hand, while less talented than his
brother, has become a famous and wealthy surgeon. He is a selfish and
egocentric man who sacrificed everything and everyone to his drive for
success. At the same time, he is also an extension of Quentin and Leduc.
A few years earlier he suffered a mental breakdown and has come to
realize that because of his terror of failure he has, in effect, murdered
life. He returns now, having seemingly and at long last conquered his
guilt, to reestablish a relationship with his brother, who he believes has
found a more meaningful existence through a life of self-sacrifice.[14]

As the two men confront each other—and their past, which is presented in all of its accumulation through the furniture of the set—each
of them comes to discover that he represents a different aspect of the
same dilemma. Miller puts this very clearly in his production note to
the play, where he writes:

> As the world now operates, the qualities of both brothers are necessary to
> it; surely their respective psychologies and moral values conflict at the heart
> of the social dilemma. The production must therefore withhold judgment
> in favor of presenting both men in all their humanity and from their own
> viewpoints. Actually, each has merely proved to the other what the other
> has known but dared not face. At the end, demanding of one another what
> was forfeited to time, each is left touching the structure of his life.[15]

The structure of life which both men are forced to accept as their own
is a structure in which all of the positive aspects of otherness have been
excluded. They have touched neither each other nor the world because
they were not brought up to believe in one another but to succeed. In
developing this idea, Miller is doing much more than challenging the
whole American money ethos as he had in *Death of a Salesman*. This is

---

[14] "The actor playing Walter must not regard his attempts to win back Victor's
friendship as mere manipulation. From entrance to exit, Walter is attempting to put
into action what he has learned about himself, and sympathy will be evoked for him
in proportion to the openness, the depth of need, the intimation of suffering with
which the role is played." (Author's Production Note, *The Price*, p. 117)
[15] *The Price*, p. 117.

a play about absence, and the absence at the core of the play is the absence of love. There is nothing at the center of these men's lives, and there never has been; there is nothing at the center of Victor and Esther's relationship; there was nothing at the center of Walter's broken marriage; there was nothing at the center of their parents' relationship or in the sons' relationships to their parents. The great revelation of the play is spoken by Walter, when he says to Victor:

> It's that there was no love in this house. There was no loyalty. There was nothing here but a straight financial arrangement. That's what was unbearable.[16]

The whole *agon* between the brothers hinges on the assumption that "there is such a thing as a moral debt." Both men have justified everything that they have or have not done, as well as everything that has or has not happened to them in terms of this imperative. This is particularly true of Victor. His wasted twenty-eight years are his moral capital, and, until Walter finally forces him to acknowledge that in his heart he knows he has been living a lie, he has managed to believe that this capital was backed by the hard currency of self-sacrifice. This feeling explains both his insistent need to demand "a price" and also his need for vengeance even if it costs him (symbolically) his life. Certainly Esther has supported him in this belief, for their empty life together would have had absolutely no meaning or justification if there were no valid moral indebtedness. Walter, on the other hand, realized during his illness that he had paid the price and why he had done so. Now, struggling with his guilt, he comes—again with a reasoning similar to Leduc's—to act:

> I've learned some painful things, but it isn't enough to know; I wanted to act on what I know.

What Miller is challenging, however, is the whole idea of moral debt based on "price." For whenever people try to relate to each other in terms of the price to be paid, they will always get less than they bargained for; the price is never enough. Both Walter and Victor have been wrong; in life there can be no question of success or failure, or "I gave more than you." This is the significance of Gregory Solomon, the used furniture dealer who has come to purchase the junk heap of their past.
  Solomon, the wise man, is one of Miller's greatest theatrical creations. Not because, as so many critics have noted, he is Miller's first major

---

[16] *The Price*, p. 109.

comic figure, but rather because he represents an expanded view of life
that incorporates all of the most significant ideas and attitudes that the
playwright has been working with for almost a decade. Solomon's wisdom, simply stated, is that it is silly for the brothers to worry about the
price, because it will always be fair. Whether the final price offered for
the furniture is $1,100, $3,500, $12,000, $25,000, or $2.50 really doesn't
matter since, as he says, the price of the used furniture of our lives is
only a viewpoint, and we can never deal with life's real issues in terms
of *quid pro quo.* The fairness of Solomon's price is underscored by such
lines as "I'm not sixty-two years in the business by taking advantage,"
"I used to be president" (of an Appraisers' Association), "I made it all
ethical," "Listen, before me was a jungle—you wouldn't laugh so much.
I put in all the rates, what we charge, you know—I made it a profession,
like doctors, lawyers—used to be it was a regular snake pit. But today,
you got nothing to worry—all the members are hundred percent ethical."
To a man who has spent most of his ninety years picking up the pieces
of other people's lives, usually in times of misfortune, the price is a
minor matter. "What happens to people is always the main element to
me." This is the source of Solomon's remarkable vitality. Even at his
advanced age, he cannot help becoming involved again; just as he entered into his fourth marriage when he was in his seventies.

In addition to pointing up the fact that paying the price is finally
irrelevant—both the brothers have paid a heavy price, but so what?—
Solomon's presence serves two other important functions. One of these
is especially clear in the second half of the play. After dominating a
good share of the first act, the old man is shunted to the bedroom shortly
after Walter arrives on the scene, and the second act is primarily devoted
to the conflict of the brothers. But Solomon does not disappear altogether, and each of his entrances is significant. In effect, he serves to
keep the brothers honest; his interruptions deter them from arriving at
false or illusory solutions.

He first returns when they seem to have touched each other by recalling their parents as they were before the Crash (p. 76). This is a
purely sentimental response, and later revelations in the play make it
clear that no renewed bond could ever be built upon such roseate memories. After Walter takes him back to the bedroom, this possibility is
never raised again. Solomon's second appearance occurs just when Walter
is offering Victor an administrative job at the hospital (p. 86). This, too,
is an illusory solution, because it reveals not only Walter's great sense of

guilt, but his total inability to take in what has really been gnawing at Victor during all the years since their separation. For the same reasons that Victor cannot go along with Walter's idea to use the furniture as a tax deduction, he finds it intolerable to be offered this "gift" of a more meaningful job. He is unquestionably right that he is not suited for the job; but even if he were it would not lessen his resentment, only enhance it. Solomon's third entrance (p. 93) comes just as the brothers think they are about to face the "dreadful" moment of truth. I believe that his remarks at this point, to the effect that the government may catch up with them, really apply as much to the revelations that are soon to follow as to the legality of Walter's proposition. Finally, he returns when the brothers have actually reached the bedrock of truth (p. 112) in the middle of Walter's last speech:

> *Walter—humiliated by her. He is furious. He takes an unplanned step toward the door:* You quit; both of you. *To Victor as well:* You lay down and quit, and that's the long and short of all your ideology. It is all envy!
> *Solomon enters, apprehensive, looks from one to the other:*
> And to this moment you haven't the guts to face it! But your failure does not give you moral authority! Not with me! I worked for what I made and there are people walking around today who'd have been dead if I hadn't. Yes. *Moving toward the door, he points at the center chair.* He was smarter than all of us—he saw what you wanted and he gave it to you! *He suddenly reaches out and grabs Solomon's face and laughs.* Go ahead, you old mutt —rob them blind, they love it! *Letting go, he turns to Victor.* You will never, never again make me ashamed! *He strides toward the doorway.*

This is a painful moment, but it is the only one that is worth something. In a symbolic sense, Solomon has helped them to arrive at this point by preventing them from settling for anything less.

As a character, Solomon is much more than a Pirandellian raisonneur whose dramatic function is to lead the protagonists (and the audience) to a new kind of understanding of their situation. The reason Solomon is the "wise man" about the play's central issues is that he has experienced them himself. He does know. His other major function may be discerned in the numerous references to his daughter's suicide which are woven throughout the play. The first time his daughter is mentioned (p. 37), her suicide is not brought up, but simply the fact that she had nothing significant to believe in. ("You're worse than my daughter! Nothing in the world you believe, nothing you respect—how can you live?") In equating Victor with his daughter, he is prefiguring the emptiness of

the policeman's life, for Victor neither believes in nor respects the self-
sacrifice he has used to justify his choice of what to him is a failed life.
(There *need* be nothing wrong with twenty-eight years of dedicated service to the police force!) And when Solomon continues, pointing out that
if you cannot believe in the life you are living, then "my friend—you're
a dead man!" the parallel to Victor is even more apparent.

Later, Solomon reveals that his daughter committed suicide fifty years
ago (p. 47) and openly admits that he has been haunted by this act all
his life. "And you can't help it, you ask yourself—what happened? What
happened? Maybe I could have said something to her . . . maybe I *did*
say something . . . it's all . . ." As his voice fades into momentary silence, we cannot help being reminded of similar agonizing queries in the
two previous plays.

The daughter is not mentioned again until the very end of the play.
At this point Solomon is paying Victor "the price" for the furniture, and
Esther has just lamented the brothers' failure to make a meaningful
contact ("So many times I thought—the one thing he wanted most was
to talk to his brother, and that if they could—But he's come and he's
gone. And I still feel it—isn't that terrible? It always seems to me that
one little step more and some crazy kind of forgiveness will come and
lift up everyone. When do you stop being so . . . foolish?"). Solomon
replies:

> I had a daughter, should rest in peace, she took her own life. That's nearly
> fifty years. And every night I lay down to sleep, she's sitting there. I see her
> clear like I see you. But if it was a miracle and she came to life, what would
> I say to her? *He turns back to Victor, paying out.*[17]

Solomon has lived life fully, and he is also a wise man. The essential
lesson he has learned is that the murder/suicide in each of us can never
adequately explain or justify what we have done or have not done to
others. We must accept our guilt knowing that it is just, but also with
the full awareness that any attempt to seek revenge on others for the
guilt for which we are responsible is to choose the road of nothingness.

As I said earlier, otherness is an ambiguous reality. Unless we can
accept a person as another we can never really touch him, and without
such contact we can never touch the world of all men. Yet since we can
never really know another, he will always be the Jew, the stranger.
("Each man has his Jew; it is the other.") Here is the absurd contradic-

---

[17] *The Price*, p. 114.

tion that the intellect can never resolve. To live in relationship is to make the Kierkegaardian leap—knowing that none of us would ever know what to say to Solomon's daughter if she were to return, but knowing also that it is irrelevant to worry about "the price." This is the meaning of Solomon's laughter as the curtain falls. Life may be an absurd joke, but it is the only life we have. Arthur Miller may or may not have read Ugo Betti's *The Gambler*, but I think that—at least at this point in time—he would agree with the spirit expressed by Betti in these lines:

> To believe in God is to know that all the rules will be fair and that there will be wonderful surprises. (*The Gambler*, Act II)

V

In an essay written a few years ago,[18] I remarked that the dominant characteristic of the American theatre during the first half of the 1960's was its passionate commitment to the business of self-scrutiny. Today, as we come closer to the end of the decade, there is no new evidence that convinces me to alter that view. All of our serious playwrights have responded to the violent disturbances of our national life—Vietnam, racism, urban problems, assassination and murder, poverty in the midst of plenty—by seeking to give definition to the soulscape which forms our planetary and spiritual horizons. No one has been more involved in this search than Arthur Miller.

In his adaptation of Ibsen's *An Enemy of the People,* Miller described Dr. Stockman as one who "might be called the eternal amateur—a lover of things, of people, of sheer living, a man for whom the days are too short, and the future fabulous with discoverable joys. And for all this most people will not like him—he will not compromise for less than God's own share of the world while they have settled for less than Man's." Although I am sure he has no such Promethean ambitions, Mr. Miller might well have been describing himself. Certainly no modern playwright writes with such moral earnestness and has a greater sense of social responsibility.

In a time when so many playwrights are dealing with modern man's isolation and loneliness, Miller, without denying either the loneliness or

[18] *Times Literary Supplement,* November 25, 1965.

the isolation, is convinced that "the world is moving toward a unity, a unity won not alone by the necessities of the physical developments themselves, but by the painful and confused reassertion of man's inherited will to survive." His passionate concern that attention be paid to the aspirations, worries, and failures of all men—and, more especially, of the little man who is representative of the best and worst of an industrialized democratic society—has resulted in plays of great range and emotional impact. For the past quarter of a century a disturbingly large percentage of the plays written for the American theatre have tended to be case histories of all forms of social and psychological aberration. For Arthur Miller, who has been a major figure during the whole period, this has not been the case; he has insisted with a continually broadening range that courage, truth, trust, responsibility, and faith must be the central values of men who would (as they must) live together.

Though the dominant tone of the theatre in the mid-twentieth century is despair, Miller continually demands more; he seeks a "theatre in which an adult who wants to live can find plays that will heighten his awareness of what living in our times involves." Miller's own sense of involvement with modern man's struggle to be himself is revealed in his own growth as an artist and has made him one of the modern theatre's most compelling and important spokesmen.

Arthur Miller: The Development of a Political Dramatist in America

by Eric Mottram

Although some of the stage sets for his plays may have suggested the contrary, Arthur Miller's theatre has never been experimentally avant-garde: from his beginnings he has aimed at a critical clarification of the already existent attitudes of liberal-minded American theatregoers. His plays are written for and largely from the point of view of a man whose attitudes are not radical and innovatory but puzzled, confused and absolutely resolved not to break with his fellow countrymen. He has maintained his theatre as nearly popular as an intellectual playwright may and still be tolerated on Broadway since the 1940's. Two of his plays were included in the opening season of the Lincoln Centre repertory company, the New York approximation to an initiatory national theatre, where he functioned as the official contemporary dramatist. *After the Fall* and *Incident at Vichy* seemed to satisfy no one at the time, and yet in these plays once again Miller dealt with his local themes of faith and meaning within the confused national and personal life of America, and dealt with them without abstractions which might call for a re-thinking of the Great Society.

Miller once remarked: "I can't live apart from the world." Yet his plays dramatize the ways in which a man alienates himself from his society and fights to get back into it. Until his most recent play, the structure of that society goes uncondemned and unanalysed, taken as if it were an unchangeable artefact. The weight of action falls cruelly on the individual within the fixed, powerful society which fails to support him at his moment of need and remains, as he falls, monolithically im-

"Arthur Miller: The Development of a Political Dramatist in America" by Eric Mottram. From *American Theatre* (Stratford-Upon-Avon Studies No. 10), [London: Edward Arnold (Publishers) Ltd., 1967], edited by John Russell Brown and Bernard Harris. Reprinted by permission of Eric Mottram and Edward Arnold (Publishers) Ltd.

23

movable. "Evil" is those social pressures which conflict with an equally vaguely defined individual integrity in the hero or heroine. But critical though he is of American, perhaps Western, values, Miller finally has come to believe that "evil" is really the natural cruelty of human nature seen, not as a product of historical social structures, but as inevitable data. The dilemma of his last two plays lies here in a nagging circularity which makes his work typical of frustrated American liberalism.

Part of the problem may well be the nature of Broadway where Miller has found success. Commenting on the high cost of seats in Broadway theatres and the influence this has on the composition of audiences, Harold Clurman ventured the opinion that this public is not genuinely concerned with politics: "The ordinary American might define politics as something to do with elections and graft . . . something to which one lends oneself for a few minutes a day on TV, or can be disposed of by a cursory glance at the headlines and by gossip about 'personalities.' Politics is a sort of sport and no one except a politician needs to devote himself to it" (*The Nation*, 25 October, 1965). The implication is that Americans are not concerned with the means of change in their society. American theatre responded politically to the Depression and New Deal years but, after World War II, political theatre for the majority was the televised McCarthy trials. Today the cry is "dissent!"; but as Clurman observes:

we hardly know what to dissent from except such enormities as totalitarianism, the insults of individual powers, narcotics and teenage killers. Dissent usually involves criticism of our country, than which there is none better on earth. Dissent, moreover, smacks of softness towards foreign ideologies. We had enough of that in the Thirties.

Clurman's irony yields, however, to nostalgia for the theatres of the 'thirties which brought forth a handful of decent plays that did not divorce entertainment from daily life. Arthur Miller began his career in the Federal Theatre, a state-aided post-Depression project created by the Roosevelt programme of national recovery. He joined this group just before its conclusion, but he has remained in the public arena of social theatre. In 1965 he was elected the first American international president of PEN, and the choice was supported by the Yugoslavs and popular with the Russians. The following November he refused an invitation to the White House in protest against President Johnson's Vietnam policy. Now in his fiftieth year, Miller writes: "When the guns boom, the arts die and this law of life is far stronger than any law man may devise": a woolly publicity statement, no doubt, but the protest was true enough and based concretely on the United States' rejection of Hanoi peace proposals. Yet, as part of the White House celebration of the signing of the Arts and Humanities Act, Mildred Dunnock read two passages from *Death of a Salesman.*

In his plays, Miller's restless social conscience moves towards the logical nihilism of *Incident at Vichy*—from the sociality of the 'thirties, through the confused liberalism of the 'forties, to the bewildered emptiness of the 'sixties. The plays are the barometer of his audience, measuring through his own sense of the pressures of the last quarter of a century. Before the House Un-American Activities Committee in June, 1956, he admitted that he protested against the outlawing of the Communist party, opposed the Smith Act (whereby it is an offence to advocate the overthrow of the U.S. Government by force), and refused to name people he had seen at Communist writers' meetings seventeen years earlier. The Committee's attorney read a revue piece on which Miller had collaborated in 1939, which represented the Committee, already investigating un-American activities, as an insane Star Chamber, torturing its helpless victims:

Attorney. Well, Mr. Miller?
Miller. But that was *meant* to be a farce.

At this stage in his career, Miller met American establishment society head-on and won a tactical victory—and a dangerous position in the series of moves he began in his youth.

His father's image, as a man and an American, diminished for the boy when the Depression brought poverty to the family. The rich clothing manufacturer in decline became the youth's symbol of national experience. The middle-class young man drove trucks, unloaded cargo at the docks, waited at hotel tables and studied journalism at Michigan University by working at night on the *Michigan Daily* for an income that was supplemented from the National Youth Administration and a few prizes for writing (he gained three drama prizes before graduation in 1938). The Theatre Guild National Award of 1937 he shared with Tennessee Williams. Money came later from radio scripts. Rejected by the army in the war (for unsteady knees), he worked as a fitter in the Brooklyn Navy Yard and then on the script for a training film, an experience written up in *Situation Normal* (1944). Hollywood did not attract him, and in 1944 he wrote *Focus,* a novel-study of anti-semitism. Miller's first play on Broadway concerned luck, a theme which haunts American literature since the Civil War because it involves deciding where the responsibility for success or disaster lies—with man, society or God, universal will, a determinist force in Nature or history.

There were difficulties: the American hero of such a fate drama could not be a king or a prince; and the idea of gods playing gloomy tricks with Americans contradicts the Constitution. But fate crept in by the back door, held open by liberal confusion. O'Neill said: "I am not interested in the relations of man to man, but of man to God," and Miller quotes this in his article "The Shadows of the Gods," refusing its implications: "I too had a religion, however unwilling I was to be so backward. A religion with no gods but with godlike powers. The powers of economic crisis and political imperatives which had twisted, torn, eroded, and marked everything and everyone I laid eyes on." He admires Tennessee Williams for his "long reach and a genuinely dramatic imagination . . . his aesthetic valour, so to speak . . . his very evident determination to unveil and engage the widest range of causation conceivable to him. He is constantly pressing his own limit . . . He possesses the restless inconsolability with his solutions which is inevitable in a genuine writer." Both writers know that analysis itself is short-measure: "ultimately someone must take charge; this is the tragic dilemma." We are trying ridiculously to create an Oedipus:

> whose catastrophe is private and unrelated to the survival of his people, an "Oedipus" who cannot tear out his eyes because there will be no standards by which he can judge himself; an "Oedipus," in a word, who on learning of his incestuous marriage, instead of tearing out his eyes, will merely wipe away his tears thus to declare his loneliness.

But somehow, for Miller, his characters must have a universalized validity. Leslie Fiedler comments on this problem with accuracy: he sees Miller as one of those Jewish-American writers who "creates crypto-Jewish characters, characters who are in habit, speech, and condition of life typically Jewish-American, but who are presented as something else— general-American say, as in *Death of a Salesman* . . . Such pseudo-universalizing represents, however, a loss of artistic faith, a failure to remember that the inhabitants of Dante's Hell or Joyce's Dublin are more universal as they are more Florentine or Irish" (p. 91).

The Man Who Had All the Luck is too pat an exposure of a struggle for success in a Middle West town. The mechanism is too obvious. But the action does ask the typical Miller questions, here at the outset of his career: do men control their fate at all or are they "jellyfish moving with the tide" (which is exactly Dreiser's initiatory query in his Cowperwood series)? Do men "get what they desire" or are they helpless victims of some indifferent force, god or providential power? Already Miller's answers are "yes" and "no" together. The man who had all the luck believes that "good luck" brought him business success, killed his girl friend's bullying father in an accident, and gave him a healthy son. His friends fail simply through "bad luck." Realization that fate rules indiscriminately threatens to drive him mad, and he is happier when he is made to understand that his own ability and careful action were involved. Miller equates caution with goodness and equivocates thoroughly over the central issues he raises.

All My Sons, based on a true story, presents Chris Keller, the returned army officer, rejecting Joe Keller's criminal irresponsibility, whether he is his father or not. The father shoots himself once the son knows the truth. He accepts his fate, but so does the son. In a position of wartime responsibility, Joe had allowed 120 cracked engine-heads to go from his factory into P40 aircraft, directly causing their pilots' deaths, the slaughter of his own son's comrades in battle. He allowed his subordinate and next-door neighbour, Deever, to be imprisoned and disgraced for his own criminality, but at the age of 61 he comes to realize that those pilots were "all my sons," and commits suicide—but with nothing to say about Deever. Keller's life is a waste: he forfeits his son's love and his own good name for a public business ethic which is strictly unusable in private, family and neighbourhood life. The business ethic puts financial and social self-interest first, and social responsibility and purpose second. The war exposes the radical moral division: Joe's horror at his own crime is insignificant beside his larger irresponsibility to "a universe of people."

This plot is presented through unstylized conversation, with a minimum of stage devices, symbolism or heightened language. The terror emerges from the ordinariness of the scene in which moral sense is smothered and self-accusation follows enlightenment. Miller wants Joe Keller to be innocent in so far as he is "the uneducated man for whom there is still wonder in the many commonly known things, a man whose judgments must be dredged out of experience and a peasant-like common sense." He is to be a Miller archetype, in fact. His son, Chris, is the

other archetype Miller will constantly return to: the moral idealist taking
his cue from the moral gyroscope of inner-direction, to use Riesman's
term. He retains his capacity to love in spite of capitalist and war experience. The mother has Joe's "talent for ignoring things": she is a fatalistic
horoscope-reader who believes God is that "certain things have to be, and
certain things can never be." The surrounding neighbourhood, the nu-
cleus of society, thought Deever deserved his fate and that Keller was
"smart": up to a point, the social ethic condones things as they are. Ann
—the sweetheart of Keller's other son, Larry (airpilot presumed dead in
action)—will marry Chris, whom she resembles in moral idealism, but she
is Deever's daughter. Her father's crime against humanity is simply an
unforgivable act, father or not. Keller hypocritically puts a case for
Deever based on the convention of the "little man" alone and afraid,
caught in the business machine. The past, in Miller's Ibsen manner,
reaches into the present and overcomes the future. Chris tells Ann, "we're
going to live now!" and the play proceeds to destroy that confidence.

The example of responsibility is the men of Chris's company dying
for each other, and this is opposed to the "ratrace" exemplified by the
Keller business. Miller's moral centre is a slightly old-fashioned expression of the notion that property is a crime:

> when you drive that [new car] you've got to know that it came out of the
> love man can have for a man, you've got to be a little better because of that.
> Otherwise what you have is really loot, and there's blood on it.

Like the Proctors, in the later *Crucible*, Chris and Ann have to have
their love and respect tested in the fire of public events. A minor character criticizes Chris—"he wants people to be better than it's possible
to be"—and insists that compromise is necessary. Keller believes that he
betrayed the pilots for his family and, especially, for his son, "my only
accomplishment." In Act II, in this struggle of fathers and sons, Deever's
son George determines to apply the law to release his father by condemning Keller. He resists family softening and the Mother's accusation
of hardness and self-destruction. Miller's point is that the community
ethic rests on moral chaos, and at the height of the family cosiness he
allows Keller to betray his faked life. The Mother is made to blurt out
her truth: Larry must be alive because if he is not, Joe Keller killed
him. As Chris's love for his father vanishes, possibly too abruptly, Miller
makes Keller give his central plea for justice:

what could I do! I'm in business, a man is in business; a hundred and twenty cracked, you're out of business; you got a process, the process don't work you're out of business . . . what could I do, let them take forty years, let them take my life away? . . . Chris, I did it for you, it was a chance and I took it for you. (p. 115)

This is the root of the action and Chris turns on his father:

For me! Where do you live, where have you come from? . . . Is that as far as your mind can see, business? . . . Don't you have a country? Don't you live in the world? What the hell are you? You're not even an animal, no animal kills his own, what are you?

But Miller makes Keller say before his suicide only "I'm his father and he's my son, and if there's something bigger than that I'll put a bullet in my head" (p. 120). He is therefore finally a martyr to a false ethic of family and business sentimentality. Chris believes in a code of traditional honour older than America and capitalism. Keller can cry, "a man can't be Jesus in this world!"; but the answer is that Christ only wants people to be better and responsible, and the play concludes in a suicide of shame and hopelessness without the slightest suggestion as to how American society could be changed to prevent these circumstances endlessly repeating.

Death of a Salesman takes up the battle of fathers and sons and removes the argument from the clear-cut war case to the everyday case of Willy Loman destroying himself for business and family. The long run of this play on Broadway was remarkable considering its sombre pathos which offers no release from tension and sadness. Basically it is an expressionist play of degradation, and in spite of one feeble question put to the audience, once again Miller leaves the conflict between a man and his society hanging fire between suicide and an intolerably unchanging world. He scores his points, with undoubted success, through a system of language which repeats ordinary catch-phrases and shared jargon, manipulated to cover the facts. Where *All My Sons* concentrated its retributive action into fifteen hours, *Death of a Salesman* uses flashbacks within an expressionist set in order to present the contents of the sixty-year-old hero's mind as he draws towards suicide after self-perceived wasted life. Again, the waste is not countered with any suggestion of radical change in the society's ethic which caused it. We are offered only the wife's cry of warning to her two sons in Act I:

I don't say he's a great man. Willy Loman never made a lot of money.
His name was never in the paper. He's not the finest character that ever
lived. But he's a human being, and a terrible thing is happening to him. So
attention must be paid. He's not to be allowed to fall into his grave like an
old dog. Attention, attention must finally be paid to such a person. You
called him crazy . . . a lot of people think he's lost his—balance. But you
don't have to be very smart to know what his trouble is. The man is exhausted . . . A small man can be just as exhausted as a great man. (pp. 162–
63)

But what terrible thing has happened to Loman, what attention must
be paid, what has exhausted him, and what kind of balance has he lost?
He is not a murderer like Keller, but he too reaches the shocking
realization that his life has been work and for nothing. Loman has been
unable to learn that business ethics, the morality of his work-community,
oppose the traditions he assumed were still in action: the personal ethic
of honour, the patriarchal nature of a basically benevolent society and
family, and neighbourhood relations. He speaks the very language of
that acquisitive society, without hypocrisy, the terminology of the world
which throws him off-balance.

Miller presents a fairly full context for the suicide, but he cannot
show his hero attaining any profound understanding of his end. Loman's
father made flutes and sold them himself throughout the States in the
self-made businessman's manner. Loman's brother Ben is the next stage:
the man self-made outside America: "Why, boys, when I was seventeen
I walked into the jungle, and when I was twenty-one I walked out. [*He
laughs.*] And by God I was rich" (p. 157). In stage three, the jungle is
New York, the American city, where a man stays, burdened by a house
overtopped by skyscrapers, household payments on equipment with
built-in obsolescence, mortgage and insurance worries, and a built-in
belief that the competitive society is life itself at its best. As in *All My
Sons*, the son penetrates some of the father's illusions. Biff Loman tried
life on a Texas ranch but remained inhibited by his father's standards.
In a flashback Miller presents the father-son relationship as a manic
cult of youthful athletic prowess operated at the expense of maturity,
with Dad as the great pal and Mother the source of binding love. Miller's
criticism, as far as it goes, emerges from the conflict between youth and
age, private and public life, optimism and suicidal despair. Like Keller,
Loman perceives he has "accomplished" nothing, but it is still "the
greatest country in the world" even if "personal attractiveness" gets you

nowhere. He perceives that "the competion is maddening," but he refers here to the uncontrolled birthrate only. His second son, Happy, is also a salesman, already lost to booze and sex, obsessed with the empty word "future," always on his lips.

But the boys are only in their thirties, and at least Biff knows he is still "like a boy," as his father is, locked in the national myth of youthfulness. Once a Loman's energy is drained by his society he is thrown aside, in this case casually sacked by the son of the man who has been his boss for thirty-four years. He protests: "You can't eat the orange and throw the peel away—a man is not a piece of fruit!" He is wrong, but Miller cannot find anyone to help him. The language itself blocks understanding: "well-liked," "create personal interest," making "an apperance," "knocking 'em cold." The appalling hypnotic power of such repeated terms is the action of a deadly stifling of vitality in the name of optimism. Loman's exhaustion is the tiredness of empty buoyancy, of feeling "kind of temporary" about himself. His wife provides loving despair; Biff knows he is a "fake."

Lost honour and comradeship permeate Miller's work. His men live on a vision they cannot make work. Loman lives in a world where his sons are Adonises, with Biff on the football field in a golden helmet "like a young god—something like that. And the sun, the sun all around him." But the boys' old school friend Bernard, who worked at his books, is now defending a case in the Supreme Court, and it is Charley, his father and Loman's old friend, who says outright that personal relations and codes of honour are meaningless now:

> Why must everybody like you? Who liked J. P. Morgan? Was he impressive? In a Turkish bath he'd look like a butcher. But with his pockets on he was very well liked. (p. 192)

But Loman is beyond advice and change; in fact he is dead already, believing that, through his insurance, he is worth more, in cash, dead than alive, and this at least would atone for his cruelty to his wife and betrayal of his sons. It now comes out that Biff lost the will to live when he saw his father with a tart, and lost the will to pass his exams: "we never told the truth for ten minutes in this house" (p. 216). They are all victims of a "phoney dream" and it is the American dream.

Happy still believes his father was right, even after the suicide, and many of Miller's audience must have agreed in their hearts. But Loman is what happens to an ordinarily uneducated man in an unjust competitive society in which men are victimized by false gods. His fate is not tragic. There is nothing of the superhuman or providential or destined in this play. Everyone fails in a waste of misplaced energy. A travelling salesman is on record with a good criticism of the play: "that damned New England territory never was any good." But other men made another criticism (in the phone calls, letters and telegrams Miller received): "I saw your play. I've just quit my job. What do I do now?" One man said, "Why didn't Willy Loman go to the Household Finance Corporation and solve all his problems?" Two large corporations asked Miller to address their sales meetings. Earlier, *All My Sons* had been picketed by the Catholic Veterans and the American Legion. Times change. But Miller's message is ambiguous: Loman may be "uneducated" and the victim of a "vulgar idea of success," but the system which fails him is "inevitable," as inevitable as the world of Dreiser's Clyde Griffith.

Miller presents *Death of a Salesman* and *All My Sons* in a spirit of puzzled, anguished analysis but does not suggest to his Broadway audience that anything so radical as revolutionary change in American terminal society might be necessary. In his essay, "Tragedy and the Common Man," contemporary with *Death of a Salesman*, he repudiates the idea that "the tragic mode is archaic" owing to the absence of socially elevated heroes and the advent of habits of scepticism and analysis. He vaguely refers to modern psychiatric uses of Oedipus and Orestes complexes which "apply to everyone in similar emotional situations." This acceptance of muddled notions of Greek tragedy and modern psychology leads him to plump for that old stand-by for the American liberal, "the individual," once agin comfortably unexamined:

> I think tragic feeling is evoked in us when we are in the presence of a character who is ready to lay down his life, if need be, to secure one thing— his sense of personal dignity. From Orestes to Hamlet, Medea to Macbeth, the underlying struggle is that of the individual attempting to gain his "rightful" position in his society.

But if the hero dies at his own hand, with the sense of waste and bewilderment still entire within him, who can now be interested in anything but the chance of changing the values of the society that brings him to that degradation? The hero's challenge today threatens the hierarchical determinations of the controllers of society and their representatives, the play's backers and audiences.

Tragedy is the consequence of a man's total compulsion to evaluate himself justly.

But if that evaluation must take place in a structure of injustice, of subservience as a wage-slave, of self-help within an economic structure which limits or denies the hero's self-fulfilment, and of an ideology which determines only that some men are more equal than others, then you have the dilemma of Miller's plays: not tragedies but plays of partial awakening to fate before a conclusion in suicidal waste. Miller believes that the tragic flaw (itself a misreading of classical theory) is not weakness but "inherent unwillingness to remain passive." The passive, therefore, are flawless and the majority are passive; Miller realizes accurately that the "terror" of this kind of life lies in "the total onslaught by an individual against the seemingly stable cosmos surrounding us . . . the 'unchangeable' environment." But surely the "evil" lies in those who perpetuate this environment, passively or actively. If the plot is not to be simply a mocking of the non-passive man, it must show a real chance of heroism and change. This Miller fails to do. "The thrust for freedom," he says, "is the quality in tragedy which exalts. The revolutionary questioning of the stable environment is what terrifies. In no way is the common man debarred from such thoughts or such action." But the common man is liable to arouse only pity as a poor fool in terror for his life unless he is allowed an understanding that his revolt is towards ends which have a specific chance of attainment. Otherwise the context is rigid sterility.

At least Miller does not degrade human life in the manner of Broadway psycho-drama which claims that self-analysis cures everything, or of the social melodrama which claims that economic change predicates total human change. He wants theatre to present "a balanced concept of life" in which the hero's need is "to wholly realize himself" without the questioning author preaching revolution. Consequently, when Loman is betrayed by the myths and ethic of his society, all we are given is his wife's pitiful cry: "Attention, attention must finally be paid to such a person."

Miller says *The Crucible,* his next play, concerns pure evil. He removes his action now to the seventeenth century and uses a language which forfeits the contemporary tensions of *Death of a Salesman* for the jargon of a theocracy. Related to contemporary McCarthy hysteria, *The*

Crucible reconstructs the Salem witch trials of 1692, and therefore requires a lengthy exposition to establish the community's ethic, law and attitude towards non-conformity and truth-telling before the moral climaxes of Acts III and IV. The characters are figures in a morality play, as usual in Miller, but for the first time he shows insecure authority violently enacting its neurosis against the man who says "No" to the law and "Yes" to his inner-directing conscience.

The action spreads from spring to autumn and needs the sense of accumulating time for its development. There are no flashbacks to dissipate suspense. The theme of masculine honour is there at the outset in the Reverend Parris' fear for his "good name" and "character" in the community he needs to win. But his daughter appears to be under a witch's spell and the old man fears for his reputation and power if his house is claimed to be devil-haunted. In fact the "spell" is part of a clever fraud perpetrated by his seventeen-year-old niece, Abigail, who has intimidated a group of Salem girls, playing witchcraft in the woods, into denouncing John Proctor, a good man whom she seduces without much difficulty. The teenagers challenge these early adult Americans and neither side will admit their fraud and fear. Gradually girls and adults believe in the magic and act on their beliefs, even though they involve torturing, burning and hanging their neighbours and friends. The law becomes a tool of acquisitive power and fearful irresponsibility.

But even Abigail cries to her uncle, "My name is good in the village! I will not have it said my name is soiled!" Part of her motivation is having seen her parents' heads battered in by Indians. She is in fact a delinquent, taking her morality from the world she knows. The centre of adult truth she attacks is John Proctor, a farmer in his middle 'thirties, and his wife Elizabeth, a development of Chris and Ann in *All My Sons,* idealists with their "own vision of decent conduct" which is not the law of the trials.

Proctor has sinned with Abigail, to use the language of the play, and it is a simple and acknowledged sin of the flesh, punished by his wife's coldness, but not a violation of his inner self. He is not a bad man but he "likes not the smell of this 'authority' " and he has factual evidence that Abigail's accusations of witchcraft are fraudulent. He is challenged by the Reverend Hale, an intellectual, proud of his specialized knowledge of the devil, a theorist whose blind ignorance of what "authority" may do with his learning drags him weeping into degradation.

Miller's encompassing theme is man judging man, a theme present in his two previous plays and reaching through to *Incident at Vichy*. Proctor's stance of judgment annoys the community and especially its judges, Danforth and Hawthorne. Proctor's wife, Elizabeth, observes:

> I do not judge you. The magistrate sits in your heart that judges you. I never thought you but a good man, John—only somewhat bewildered. (p. 265)

It is exactly the relationship between Loman and Eddie Carbone and their wives; and, as with those characters, here too the community "goes wild" around the Proctors, whose traditional conscience is exposed. John's inner-directed stability cries out against the witchcraft and injustice, in Act II:

> Is the accuser always holy now? Were they born this morning as clean as God's fingers? . . . Now the little crazy children are jangling the keys of the kingdom, and common vengeance writes the law! This is warrant's vengeance! I'll not give my wife to vengeance!

As Elizabeth is cried out for a witch, John feels himself exposed to more than society's criticism, to "God's icy wind" of which the 1692 events, like the McCarthy trials, are taken as an example. Act III presents trials and denunciation in which, in spite of Proctor's clear proof of the girls' fraud, the judges and accusers go too far and Hale awakens to his responsibility: "I have signed seventy-two death warrants; I am a minister of the Lord, and I dare not take a life without there be proof so immaculate no slightest qualm of conscience may doubt it" (p. 297). But he is over-ruled by another infallibility, that of law, and therefore Proctor is driven to attack law when he attacks the trials. In doing so he attacks authority. The trap begins to close on him and Miller comes as close as he can to supporting the individual against society without crying for revolution—which is just as well, since he himself had to appear before the House Un-American Activities Committee before long.

The play turns on a trick of authority by which Elizabeth is forced to lie for the truth. Proctor accuses Abigail of being a whore and claims his wife cannot lie. Elizabeth denies he is a lecher when he has already admitted his lechery. Now there is double proof that he has "cast away his good name." He cries out that Elizabeth "only thought to save my name!" but the girls play their witch-game again to enable the judges to bring Proctor down, until, faced by the perversity of the events against him, he says "God is dead," and damns himself finally. Hale, who has come to support him by now, rushes from the assembly denouncing the whole procedure his intellectuality had abetted. In Act IV he begs Elizabeth to make John confess and save his soul and perhaps his life. She replies "I think that be the devil's argument," which is the point at which the play recognizes the central terror of its action—the complete reversal of "good" and "evil." When John tries to make out a case for gaining his life for their joint future, she simply says: "I cannot judge you, John." Miller's point is that, since Proctor is a good man, it is vanity on his part not to recognize he is like all men whose wicked souls God sees and it is wicked not to leave his family provided for. So he may as well confess. But he switches the action here to focus fully on John's integrity: in a corrupt time, that alone is valuable. Elizabeth adamantly remarks: "John, it comes to naught that I should forgive you, if you'll not forgive yourself" (p. 323).

The following scene is a moving recognition of mutual love, respect and charity, and one of the finest Miller has written; it is the central, adult, positive humanity of the action. But what comes out of it is unconvincing. Proctor confesses (to regain his life) but will not accuse others—"I cannot judge another." Realizing his own confession will be used as an instrument against them, he tears it up: "You will not use me! It is no part of salvation that should use me!" The reason for these climactic words, which reverberate throughout American literature since the Declaration of Independence, Proctor makes into a proclamation for total integrity:

> Because it is my name! Because I cannot have another in my life! Because I lie and sign myself to lies! Because I am not worth the dust on the feet of them that hang! How may I live without my name? I have given you my soul; leave me my name! (p. 328)

He exits to his execution, accepted so voluntarily that it has suicidal qualities of self-sacrifice, even though he is a victim of the system. Proctor, unlike Keller and Loman, chooses his own fate more in the romantic lineage of promethean defiance of authority for personal honour, made secure by death. But the social structure, once again, remains intact, and it is exactly here that Jean-Paul Sartre's film script alters Miller's play.

Les Sorcières de Salem (1957), a film made to Sartre's script by Raymond Rouleau, focuses clearly from its beginning on Proctor's rebellion against the use of personal power which condemns people as sinfully corrupt by inevitable theory. Proctor's sensuality and his identification of Elizabeth with the God of prohibiting sex and the God of judgment is firmly established, and Sartre enters into a general criticism of the Protestant ethic and its relations with sex, money and power relationships. The clerics link the devil with lower-class rebelliousness against the rich and powerful—in fact the storekeeper, from whom Elizabeth wishes to buy her daughter a doll, remarks: "there are no witches among the rich." Sin is overtly sin against state authority, only made to seem sin against Jonathan Edwards' God. In such a theocracy, the borderline between actual "possession" and playacting is uncertain and some of the women in the meeting house climax are as "possessed" as the girls. An organization of "sensible citizens," both bourgeois and workers, sends a deputation to the Governor, but the lower classes come to distrust their leaders and plan among themselves to attack the gallows to forestall Proctor's execution. Danforth hopes to foil this plan by setting up the gallows inside the prison and welcomes the rebellion as an opportunity to strike at the people without remorseful conscience.

Sartre also has Abigail come to Proctor secretly, to make him confess so that they can escape to New York where no one will know of his shame; and she tempts him by threatening to become a whore in Boston. His desire for her cannot stand the idea of her body used by other men and he writes his confession accordingly. This has the effect, in the film, of making Abigail a far more sympathetic figure of passion, even when Proctor negotiates the crucial change from passion for her and love for Elizabeth. But he is hanged finally as pre-revolutionary martyr. Abigail's cries for help arouse the rebels to break into the prison but they would hang her too, as a traitor. As the final funeral cortege begins, it is Elizabeth who saves her: she quietly observes that she herself, and all of them, are guilty of the murder of Proctor. Her last words are: "Release her—she loved him," and Abigail stands shocked in a new understanding as the procession moves out of the village into the countryside.

Sartre has virtually filled out the sexual and historical details of Miller's play, which he treats as a sketch. But he also transforms Miller's characteristic despair and stress on a man's exemplary suicide into hope for social change through the murder of a hero. The film is more complex than the play, and more convincingly three-dimensional if rather more philosophically dogmatic. If the aim of such a historical drama is to analyse the present in order to change it, the deeper and wider the analysis the better. As Miller owned, *The Crucible* did not help to defeat McCarthy: "No liberal did that. The army defeated McCarthy. He attacked a general, and that was a deadly mistake" (*Guardian*, 23 January, 1965). The play's success came later, played to small non-commercial audiences already prepared to accept the liberalism it embodies.

A View from the Bridge compromises between the remote moral history of seventeenth-century Salem and contemporary Brooklyn. Eddie Carbone, like Proctor, is fearful of losing his good name and arrives, not at the suicidal hopelessness of Keller and Loman, but at the most logical death in all Miller's plays. He is killed in self-defence by the representative of the ancient traditional law which, the dramatist insists, is deeper than state social law: it is the law of honour, perpetuated in Sicily. *A View from the Bridge* is a drama of the emigrant in the New World (Carbone and Marco are Sicilians), and of the uneducated man confused by different kinds of moral law and the ambiguity of his own sexual feelings. Eddie is confronted, as in classical tragedy, with a situation for which he is unprepared, like Antony and Othello, and like Solness the masterbuilder. But Miller's hero is a carefully delineated working man, a dock labourer, to whom once again attention must be paid, in the pathos of his self-discovery.

Miller says he wanted the play to be without suspense or theatricalized life (Introduction to *A View from the Bridge*, 1960); based on a true incident, as a number of his plays are, he did not wish his action to depend on "psycho-sexual romanticism" or "mere sympathy" for a "misunderstood victim." The feeling aroused must refer to "concepts, to codes, and ideas of social and ethical importance." Suspense is there only in so far as the audience knows only too well how events will turn out; "the basic feeling would be the desire to stop this man and tell him what he was really doing to his life." That is, to educate him, and therefore the audience is presumed to be able to educate Eddie Carbone, a disastrous assumption, to say the least.

Eddie, a worker indistinguishable from his neighbourhood type, depends for his good name on being at one with the community standard. His final "I want my respect" is the heartbreaking cry of a man whose self-esteem had depended entirely on society, unlike Proctor's inner-direction. Eddie is other-directed: "his value is created largely by his fidelity to the code of his culture." That culture is European; not American but Sicilian. As in *Death of a Salesman*, the scene is Brooklyn, but here it is the dockland slum most of us only see from Brooklyn Bridge. The "fatal violation of an ancient law" is presented in naturalistic language within an expressionist set, and the action is framed, made into a detached myth, by the choral character, Alfieri, an emigrant Sicilian lawyer who partakes of the action but also speaks directly to the audience. It is he who sees, helplessly, the inevitability of Eddie's defeat, and sees two laws in conflict—the ancient pre-Greek law, the natural law as it is called, and the state law, represented by the Immigration Bureau.

But since this is Red Hook and not Sicily, in the lawyer's words "we settle for half, and I like it better. I no longer keep my pistol in my filing cabinet. And my practice is entirely unromantic" (p. 379). If you know what natural and state law are and that they conflict, and know yourself, you can work out a life. But Eddie does not know and the action takes its "bloody course," and the key word is "honour." Eddie's niece Catherine, brought up as his daughter, and nearing womanhood, is chosen out of her typists' class for a good job. This is an honour to the family, and it is also an honour to shelter two illegally emigrant Sicilians, relatives of Eddie's wife Beatrice. Community law is exemplified in the story of Vinnie Bolzano, a kid of fourteen who snitched on his uncle to the Immigration Bureau and is then turned out by family and community and never seen again. Eddie accepts the honour and the justice of this law entirely.

One of the newcomers, Marco, is an ordinary hardworking man planning to return to his family in Sicily; his brother Rodolpho is young and plans to become an American. He is a blond, handsome fellow who sings high tenor, spends his money on clothes, makes dresses for Catherine and seems totally unlike the image of normal masculinity acceptable to Eddie. Rodolpho and Catherine fall in love and intend an early marriage, and it is at this point that Eddie's repressed sexuality for his niece appears as tyrannical concern for her welfare, while his nervous sexual feeling for Rodolpho takes the form of bullying and teasing, staged excellently through a little sparring match which words could certainly not improve. Miller now shows the hand of what he calls "destiny"—"who can ever know what will be discovered? Eddie Carbone had never expected to have a destiny"—and the term means a horribly typical fate, apparently.

Miller's presentation of Eddie's inarticulate life is brilliantly written as his terrifying bewilderment increases. Alfieri tries to explain to him what is happening, but Eddie is obsessed and has no notion of the complexity of love and of social understanding. What Miller does not mention in his play is the failure of this community to become American, the chronic failure of the new society to impose an equitable social law which might over-rule the primitivism of Sicily. When Eddie gets drunk and kisses Catherine, he responds to Rodolpho's challenge by pinning his arms and kissing him as well. Miller's stage direction makes clear what he requires here: *"They are like animals that have torn at one another and broken up without a decision, each waiting for the other's mood"* (p. 423). The scene is prepared for in two ways which show what Eddie's condition is: first, Beatrice saying to him, "When am I going to be a wife again," and Eddie's refusal to discuss the matter; and secondly, his statement to Alfieri: "I mean he looked so sweet there, like an angel —you could kiss him he was so sweet." But he cannot stop the marriage, the process of natural law. Alfieri warns him:

> The law is nature. The law is only a word for what has a right to happen. When the law is wrong it's because it's unnatural, but in this case it's natural and a river will drown you if you buck it now . . . You won't have a friend in the world, Eddie! Even those who understand will turn against you, even the ones who feel the same will despise you! (p. 424)

But it is too late for such rationality to change an uneducated, passionate man like Eddie, and a man whose Americanism has not even begun. He betrays Marco and Rodolpho to the other law's representatives, the Immigration Bureau, in order to be rid of the threat to his masculinity; and immediately Sicilian law takes over, condemning his betrayal of honour. Eddie stands alone as a man who has lost his respect. In betraying the brothers he betrays himself and his cry is futile, as his appalled wife knows and accepts. Alfieri counters Marco's sense of the dishonour in not killing Carbone with another law which denies it, but Marco's reply is easy: "All the law is not in a book." Alfieri counters again with the basis of law in America: "Yes. In a book. There is no other law." But Miller leaves the argument in the air with the lawyer saying, "Only God makes justice": which justice, which law, Miller does not say. Americans must settle for half, which is civilization. But does God settle for half too? If that is the case, then tragedy is not destiny but a lack of education. The confusions are not sorted out and the play rushes on to death scenes. As he becomes the "nothing and nobody" Catherine rejects, Eddie cries "I want my name" and "I want my respect," but the only way for him to get it now is a knife-fight. The argument ends in warfare.

The animals attack each other (it is Miller's image); the law of blood in Red Hook exerts itself; Marco turns Eddie's knife back into its owner; the logic of his death is exactly within the ancient law. Miller tries to recover from this display of destiny with a liberal gesture, with Alfieri's desperate assertions: Eddie was wrong, his death useless, but we are to respect something called "himself purely" because "he allowed himself to be wholly known." So he is to be loved and mourned but "with a certain . . . alarm." That "alarm" is like the "attention" in *Death of a Salesman,* a gesture of liberal hesitation to go through with the needed radical criticism of the society which permitted and therefore encouraged this killing, this waste and this chaos. Miller's plays are a warning cry from his warm, uncertain heart detached from the economic and social implications which his head hesitates to act upon.

In February, 1960, Miller was saying that he did not in fact share Alfieri's views. He stated his dramatic aim in characteristically didactic terms: "I try to unveil a truth already known but not recognized . . . [The theatre] can help to make man more human—that is, less alone" (*Guardian,* 25 February, 1960). It is the loneliness of his heroes which produces their measure of cathartic response in the audience: the continuity from father to son breaks down; the parent generation dies in the chaos the son inherits. In 1958, Miller worked on a film script which again took up this material, focused this time on delinquent youth in New York ("Bridge to a Savage World": *Esquire,* October, 1958). The conflict of laws in *A View from the Bridge* becomes the laws of the city streets of America: the gang codes are the codes of primitive societies or clans: "When a Youth Board worker descends into the streets he is going back into human history a distance of thousands of years. Thus, it is fruitless merely to say that the delinquent must be given love and care —or the birch rod. What is involved here is a profound conflict of man's most subtle values." These boys lack contact with "civilized values" passed on from the father: "social obligation, personal duty . . . rudimentary honour." This kind of socially responsible analysis is present throughout Miller's career. He speaks of "our hunger for purpose" (*Sunday Times,* 20 March, 1960), the need to unite psychology and politics in a theatre which will "draw a whole world into one man, . . . bring a national experience to bear on an individual subject" (*Observer,* 14 October, 1956), and the failure of contemporary writers to make direct social comment in their work because of their "failure of belief in the depth of alteration that will follow if you expose an injustice" (*Observer*, 8 September, 1957).

The kind of problem he has had with the moral and political content of his plays appears clearly in "The Playwright and the Atomic World." Speaking of the reception of his plays outside America, he notes that Europeans are "more interested in the philosophic, moral and principled values of the play than we are," whereas Americans "create methods of reaching the great mass of the people." Majority acceptance pays fabulously, both financially and in terms of influence, and Miller accepts this himself, along with the criterion of judgment such a position must also hold: "the most plain aspects of usefulness." Miller wishes to write for a majority audience and his next venture was a film which concerns the transformation of popular American hero-types caused by the changes in industrial capitalist society. In *The Misfits*, the cowboy, the airman and the blonde female tamer of the West reappear divorced, alienated and bewildered, hunters of the old securities of the self at home in a society.

Miller relocates the figures of myth in economic and sexual reality. But the myth remains powerful, even in its new form. Roslyn, the anchoring symbol of sexual vitality, is part of another dream, too:

> she is all that the Jew dreams: the *shiksa,* whom his grandmother forbade him as a mate . . . played by Marilyn Monroe [at that point Miller's wife and converted to Judaism], who, under the circumstances, was bound to triumph over the male Old West, the Gentile's Saturday-matinée dream of violence and death, personified by Clark Gable, tamer of horses and women. (Leslie Fiedler, pp. 87–88)

Not only Miller was personally involved in this film; as James Goode has shown, the director, John Huston, and three of the leading actors were all, in some sense, enacting their life-roles through Miller's script. The Gable, Clift and Monroe film-images were more than actor's roles for their creators, and were part of a national mythology of the last three decades. The film is set in Reno, Nevada, "the last stop of the vanishing American innocent" (Goode, p. 92), the town of divorce and gambling, and the appropriate scene for a script concerning divorce, heroic action changed by the economic market, the evasion of society by men who wish to stay innocent, and the chances of defeat for the individual in a corrupting time. Miller's feeling for his misfitted— Keller, Loman, Proctor—reaches a curiously pure form in *The Misfits*.

There are no villains, and not even society is a villain. The main characters are good but complex and unstable, and while they undergo tests of integrity, they have nothing in them of Hemingway's unwhimpering stoics. Miller's men do not have to kill by inner necessity and they are tender to women, whom they need as Hemingway's men do not. Gay Langland works at a trade which serves his identity. When he fears he is losing Roslyn "he asserts his identity; he wants to call up his powers. When he is doing his work he feels most himself. He wants her to see the power within himself . . . the balance of disaster and hope in life is finally struck by both these people" (Goode, pp. 73 ff.).

Miller reaches, therefore, for a comedy of balance in which his main characters come to terms with each other and society; but at the end of the action Langland has still "to find some means of coming to terms with a settled existence, and face the struggle between a personal code and social cooperation." Roslyn "comes to see that the violence in man, which is the violence in all of us, can exist side by side with love." Miller explicity wished to avoid the dominating theme of American literature since the Civil War, the victimization of a man by inhuman social forces, "the documentation of defeat," accompanied by stoic "personal lament" and concluded in meaninglessness. Instead of the proletarian hero who is not "permitted to think by the literary tradition," Miller wished to create a dramatic hero of "felt knowledge," for the first time in his career.

The Misfits benefits greatly from film possibilities. The mountains on the horizon contain the wild horses; the city contains the market, divorce courts and temporary homes. Between them lie Guido's home, built by the airman for his wife who died, the rodeo where Perce Howland shows his skills at Dayton, and the arena of the sterile, neutral lake, the alkali waste to which the horses are driven and on which the men demonstrate their skill. Guido's wartime skill is used for the peacetime rounding up of mustangs, but this in itself is a mechanization of the traditional pastoral skill of men pitted against animals on the ground and hand to hoof. As the market for traditional skill retreats, airman and cowboy individualism becomes isolated into lonely bachelor games played to avoid commitment to a job for wages which reduces men to personnel. The city of divorce and money opposes the country of manhood trades and vitality; the hunters begin to search for home.

Within these versions of American traditional themes the unchanging factor is Roslyn's challenge to the three men who refuse to work for wages. Perce remains fixed in endless boyish tests for manhood at rodeos; Guido remains the liberal who "can go just so far into clinches and then just isn't there" (Goode, p. 215); only Gay achieves Roslyn's love and will try for a balance between wages and individualism which does not involve endless proving and competitiveness. This is Miller's most detailed and ambitious work, and if the film was not a masterpiece, at least Huston and the actors never betrayed the seriousness of the writer's demands. Miller's treatment, as it appears in book form, is broad and symbolic, intended to be filled out by the visual images:

> The movie springs from the way we dream. The art of cutting follows the physiology of a dream. In the dream we accept because we see it . . . The movie hits you in a very primitive part of your psychological make-up. The play, on the other hand, is built on words . . . The greatest impact will come from the image. (p. 261)

The opening shots of *The Misfits* provide the initial context for Miller's story of "the professional man": Main Street, Reno; gambling palaces; dislocated tourists and divorcees; a radio commentator boasting Reno's 411 divorces this month against Las Vegas's 391 (sponsored by Rizdale Coffee and Dream-E-Z tranquillizer); and the statue of a pioneer family. Into this scene are projected Roslyn, awaiting divorce, a girl still virtually a child in spite of her career of "interpretive dancing" in night-clubs, and the man this "golden girl" will settle for, Gay Langland, aged forty-nine:

> he sets the rhythm for whoever he walks with because he cannot follow. And he has no desire to lead . . . Homeless, he is always at home inside his shoes and jeans and shirt, and interested. (p. 13)

But this inner-direction has led to isolation, divorce and alienation from non-agrarian society. Roslyn's role is to indicate "a path through the shapeless day," and Guido's house becomes a home between city and wilderness. Guido remains locked in fear and self-pity, but he can recognize Roslyn's "gift of life." Perce is nearer the Hemingway sportsman ideal; in his late 'twenties he has become a bucking horse rider, "a resident of nowhere," a naïve and gentle boy whose sewn-up face of rodeo toughness conceals his eternally unfinished self, raw from his father's accidental death and his mother's re-marriage. He fits, in his honest lack of "remorse or excuse," only into the town without police and law whose absurdity is "so senseless as to rise to a logic, a law, a principle of destruction, as when one is knocked down by a bicycle and killed on the way to a wedding."

Perce's "pure lust for glory" is absurd, too, but it draws Roslyn's pity for his necessary trial and connects him to her own sense of glory, shown in the paddle-ball game, which, like the rodeo for Perce, resists its gambling context. Guido's "elderly" plane also redeems the absurdity of his mechanized rounding-up of the mustangs. But Miller connects Roslyn's nature with the vulnerability of the rodeo and wilderness horses, as well as with Langland's bitch, and her open fear and sympathy is further linked with the vulnerability of Langland as he drunkenly searches for his children in the Dayton crowd and falls pathetically from the hood of the car. Roslyn is associated with wild nature in the tree in Guido's garden, with the moon, and with the sky and plants. Again it is Guido who articulates her position: "You're really hooked in; whatever happens to anybody, it happens to you. That's a blessing." The crucial speech, therefore, is Langland's explanation to Roslyn why he must sell the horses for dog-food: it is deeply connected with why he, like Carbone and Proctor, must assert his manhood:

> When I started, they used a lot of them I caught. There was mustang blood pullin' all the plows in the West; they couldn't have settled here without somebody caught mustangs for them . . . It . . . just got changed around, see? I'm doin' the same thing I ever did. It's just that they . . . they changed it around.

The hesitations confirm the vagueness as to who "they" might be: Miller refuses his hero much "felt knowledge" here but gives him enough guilt to prepare for the final victory of Roslyn, her understanding that "a kind man can kill." This takes place in the film's finest scenes: the trapping and release of the mustangs, driven from the wilderness by plane and hunted on the "prehistoric lake bed" which "glistens like ice," "a picture of the moon" or "God's country." Roslyn initially sees all three men as killers, and Gay turns on her as the female type itself, that "puts the spurs to you—We ask them too much—and we tell them too little. I know—I got the marks!" But when Perce bids for Roslyn by attempting to free the trapped horses, it is Roslyn who cries out, after seeing Gay at his trade: "Oh, Perce! I don't know!" This is the turning point of the work, leading to Gay's recapture of the mustang —nearly killing himself—and his symbolic freeing of it and, thereby, himself. His lament is paradoxically his victory:

They changed it. Changed it all around. They smeared it all over with blood, turned it into shit and money just like everything else. You know that, I know that. It's just ropin' a dream now . . . Find some other way to know you're alive . . . if they got another way, any more.

Miller cannot say more than that. The end of the cowboy is not moved into the beginning of a new viable life in the West, and the end of the myths of manhood peter out in a feeble image of Roslyn and Gay driving home by a star. But Miller certainly has not, as Gerald Weales claims, "abandoned tragedy and gone the way of Broadway and Hollywood" ("The Tame and Woolly West," *The Reporter*, 2 March, 1961). Nor is it simply a matter, as Robert Hogan has it, of an indictment of both society and the family, the one "tawdry and valueless," the other "disintegrated" (p. 38). Miller's comedy of balance is more complex: the relationships between the main characters explore the needs for American hero-types to change if they are not to be alienated from surviving as men. They have to "settle for half," and refuse violence, love their women and hope for new work.

After the Fall, his next work, shows the need for this change in Miller's first intellectual professional man, a lawyer called upon to make complicated public and private decisions. In American culture and its literature, the lawyer is the central figure taming the frontier and the jungle of cities, the man whose tongue and head move America from lawlessness to the Constitution, the hero who stabilizes America in human rights based on the protection of property and the establishment of personal security.

But this play contains, notoriously, an analysis of the playwright's own recent public and private life. Shortly after shooting on *The Misfits* was completed, his wife, Marilyn Monroe, identified strongly with her role as Roslyn, announced her separation from Miller—on Armistice Day, to be precise. Clark Gable died shortly after making this, his last film, and Miss Monroe committed suicide a little later. Such events, inevitably for a playwright connected with Hollywood and Broadway, became public property, but Miller must have expected this trial. In a conversation with Huston he had defined the differences between American and English writers:

The English writer sometimes doesn't wish to identify himself with what he's writing about. He wants to be superior to it. The American writer says, "This is what I am." It's self-revelation. Some English writers don't want to give themselves away. They're more modest. . . . Certain codes of behaviour can't be converted into money and are going by the board all over the world. People degenerate when they only respond to things because there's prospect of gain or usefulness. . . . Somebody's got to say things which are profitable are not necessarily right—and to make that statement is already treasonous. (*Guardian*, 25 February, 1960)

After the Fall is Miller's self-revelation and treasonable comment on the nature of profit, necessity and American moral behaviour in mid-century, a re-working of *The Crucible* in contemporary terms into which he worked his own American confusions of public and private life. The play is also a comment on how sexuality had become "a convention" in the theatre, "a kind of shorthand through which we can appear to enter into the lives of people we're seeing." He also intended to teach Americans, traditionally fancying themselves "open-handed, on the side of justice, a little bit careless about what they buy, wasteful, but essentially good guys, optimistic," about their under-level, "the level which confronts our bewilderment, our lonely naïveté, our hunger for purpose" (*Sunday Times*, 20 March, 1960). The play concerns also the difficulty of locating "the forms of disintegration" in the personality striving for integrity. As in *The Crucible,* the analysis of the self and justice is central, but Miller is aware that since the 'forties that kind of analysis had become "a device to exclude the world. Economics, politics, these are widely regarded as mere *gaucherie*. Thus self-pity and sentimentality rush in." The leader is O'Neill once again: "his self-pity, his tortured questing, his relentless doubt, overwhelm his often stagey solutions: the other writers too often were sealed up in their plays." O'Neill exposed himself.

These ideas of self-reform as a dramatist produced Miller's first Expressionist, Strindbergian play, in which the action streams from the self-centre of the hero, and it is clear that part of the reason for this form is that Miller was "perhaps less ready to believe than he once was that this gap [between man as he is and man as he could be] can be narrowed by the passage of wise laws, the election of competent officials, or any organized gestures whatever. He is thinking more closely on man's lack of any profound concern with his true nature and his consequent failure to recognize the true nature of his inevitable bonds with others" (Allan Seager).

So, instead of enriching the social and political context of his moral actions, Miller places the burden of guilt and decision increasingly on the individual, and in that direction lies the nihilism of his two most recent plays.

Quentin, the lawyer hero of *After the Fall*, tries to recover from a world "they" changed around and from women who demanded too much. The plot takes in his Jewish family, domineering mother, Depression ruin, the McCarthy trials and their tests for personal loyalty, and the evidence of German concentration camps. Quentin cannot provide for his women because he cannot love for long, if at all, and his Jewish experience (at home and internationally, by implication) exacerbates his feeling of victimized indecision. The events and characters of this condition are presented as an autobiographical simultaneity exploring a present-tense crisis: Quentin seems to address an unseen Listener, the embodiment of the captive audience rather than an equivalent of Alfieri.

The tone is one of distressed need to confess, convince and expose, and it is hardly more interesting than the tired rehearsal of a trite series of common events, known to any American audience: the betrayals before the Congressional Investigating Committee, the disillusionment with 'thirties socialist ideology, and the broken marriages, including one to Maggie, a pop singer clearly modelled on Marilyn Monroe and a finely drawn portrait of a girl's distrust of a man with nothing but failed beliefs behind him. The failure of the play has also to do with the O'Neill type of language, a self-condemning rhetoric oscillating between the pseudo-poetic and the pseudo-analytic, all neurotic unfinished queries and platitudinously self-defeating counter-opinions. A comparison with Fellini's *8½* is completely damaging to *After the Fall*. Miller intended to show the killing power of truth and the devastation of love by the quest for power. But, unlike Fellini, Miller indulged in theories of "innocence," in the fashion of the American dream of evaded responsibility —Miller says "by innocence I mean the blindness as to one's own motives, one's own actions," and the danger which follows. The resulting play is a cancelling dialectic of truth-telling and evasion, of power against love (as crude as that), and the way out this time is no star in the sky to drive by, but Holga, the European woman who no longer believes in innocence or fall from innocence, but only in the bravery to carry on. This is not a convincing version of the traditional marriage of American innocence and European experience: it is far too schematic a solution for the isolating arrogance of a hero who has the nerve to believe himself innocent as he makes mistaken decisions. Miller believes that Quentin learns in the end "to summon courage to take life in his arms," but what can "life" mean since the action shows at least that Quentin cannot be "mature," a term defined by his first wife as "knowing that another person exists." That knowledge came through finally in *The Misfits,* but here it is merely asserted by a sterile lawyer surrounded by whispering ghosts of his past. The analogy between his betrayal of friends and wives and the planned Nazi extermination of the Jews is spurious. We are left with an American professional man's manic desire to confess exhibition-istically that he feels, really, and that he is therefore different from the callow mob of indifferents.

In reply to critics who disliked his use of Marilyn Monroe in the play, Miller wrote (*Life,* 7 February, 1964) that Maggie was not Marilyn but a symbol of "the self-destructiveness which finally comes when one views oneself as pure victim . . . —of parents, of a Puritanical sexual code and of her exploitation as an entertainer." Her suicide is the result of self-destructive forces which are externalized in the Depression, Auschwitz and McCarthyism. But the play only hints, insistently, at that kind of complexity and of the nature of guilt in America and the world in the 1960's. Quentin's effort to open Maggie's eyes to her complicity in her own destruction is intended to be "an act of love" which emerges from his own relinquishing of false innocence. But this cannot appear in the play because everything is part of Quentin's vision of himself: the form is essentially self-congratulatory. The limbo-quality of the set itself maintains a false expressionism of "no walls or substantial boundaries," symbolic "eyes" in the concentration camp tower, and the "neolithic" and "lava-like" tri-level stage and sporadic lighting intended to be "a mind questing over its own surfaces and into its depths."

After the Fall has a limited interest for its Americanisms. Here is one more hero engaged in "a series of proofs," the tests of capitalist democracy involving bravery and the conquest of the wise powerful father, dominant mother and loyal brother. Nearer to Moses Herzog than the hero of *Altona,* Quentin comes to his "bit of decision" after realizing that he alone can offer himself "justification" or "condemnation." He is "hung up," cannot "blame with confidence," indulges in fake imitation crucifixions in a hotel bedroom, and admires Holga because she decided for the Hitler assassination plot without striving for "some goddamned . . . moral victory." He throws aside expectations of "saving grace" from love or socialism or patriarchal Jewishness. But the failure of nourishment in Fitzgerald's heroes has become an embarrassing arrogance in this lawyer's exhibitionism.

His fellow-travelling senior had lied in the 'forties about the blessings of Soviet law, and lied for the Party: what he now fears is the investigation not of his opinions but his lies. But Miller's comments are feeble: "why is the world so treacherous?" and, with a silly glance at Yeats, "why do I think of things falling apart?" Act I is the rehearsal of betrayals, faithlessness and lying, the timeless breaking of illusions and repetitive movement towards inevitable hopelessness, compounded by Oedipal guilts and sterile desires to be "innocent" and to live "a straightforward life" in times of international moral chaos. Quentin emerges as the man who tried to avoid moving either way until "the web of connection between people" proves illusory during the McCarthy trials. As in all his plays, Miller wishes to fuse his public and social theme with his sexual material in order to show the failure of integrity the hero must commit. In this case, Quentin's first wife points to his basic failure: "you want a woman to provide an—atmosphere, in which there are never any issues, and you'll fly around in a constant bath of praise." A woman becomes his "instrument" instead of "a separate person," and this in turn is what he cannot bear for himself. He refuses to be identified as "a Red Lawyer" or a particular man in love with a particular woman. At this point Miller begins to develop Maggie.

Initially she has a pleasantly dotty simplicity and literalness. Her lonely vulnerability, like Roslyn's, asks to be used by men. She acts a certain self-protective "innocence" which covers her life as a woman of the world, a judge's mistress, an entertainer at conventions, and so on. She maintains a certain wholeness, symbolized by her "unbroken" hair. Like Roslyn, we are told, she is "just there," "like a tree or a cat," but society transforms love for her into "an issue." Quentin confronts her wholeness as a divided man, ignorant of morality, guilty of irresponsible feeling for his lawyer friend's suicide, and associated (by the stage-set) with the German tower. Act I ends with his querying:

> Then how do you live? A workable lie? But that comes from a clear conscience! Or a dead one. Not to see one's own evil—there's power! And rightness too!—so kill conscience.

The O'Neill-style pattern of rhetoric is typical of the nihilistic movement of *After the Fall* which exhausts itself in Act II. This begins with

Quentin's desire for power and decisive action, and "the death of love" which that implies. But most of the action concerns the deterioration of the Maggie–Quentin relationship. His respect for her provided some of the courage she needed to become a star, but, like Quentin's, her professional success barely conceals an absence of self-knowledge and integrity. She clings to him as an image of manly security until she sees him as he actually is, a man who needs her to transform: "she . . . gave me something! The power to change her!" But Maggie herself substitutes charity for love, and expects her whims about money and her extravagant ego to be taken solemnly. She temporarily becomes Quentin's Eliza Doolittle, "a kind of proof, somehow, that people can win" or be organized into self-sufficiency. But she also becomes an exploited entertainer, "some kind of joke" in the public eye. To heal this dialectic of love and power, Quentin seeks to make his love operative in the world by guiding her career. But this "power to transform somebody" ends in Maggie seeing him as protector, lawyer and promoter, and not that original man she needed, who simply "believed in me." It is towards this impasse of failure that *After the Fall* moves. Act II rushes with dreadful velocity towards Maggie's inevitable attempt at suicide and Quentin's total alienation from self and society. Maggie's cries—"I mean what is it? . . . I mean what do you want?"—remain unanswered. The ex-Party lawyer commits suicide calling Quentin's name and Quentin himself also refuses to be responsible for Maggie: "I have to survive too, honey."

The action is neither tragic nor comic but a melodrama of faithlessness. Once again, Miller drives his hero and heroine to breaking-point, as if he were obsessively tormented by the questions: how far can you trust people and at what point will they break and their faiths crumble? when is suicide the only exit? All Miller's plays concern suicide as the result of conflict between self and society; he is the significant American dramatist of alienation, the undertow of whose theatre is wilful self-destruction. *After the Fall* concludes in a paralytic tension between faith and will which destroys the cult of the individual. The agent of death is to be whisky-plus-tranquillizers, both, ironically, popular aids to living in America. Both Maggie and Quentin are obsessed with an equally popular original sin: the dominance of Mother. Quentin is the type of the modern American liberal: he seeks to condone for his sexual and moral irresponsibility by re-emphasizing the inevitability of failure and agonizing in public over his atoning self-pity. At least Miller suggests that only "God" can provide that "limitless love" which Quentin and

Maggie demand of each other. Quentin's final cry is an echo from the whole of nineteenth- and twentieth-century American literature: "Maggie, we . . . used one another!" The desire for "innocence," limitless love and power are all based on this Unpardonable Sin, the theme of both Hawthorne and O'Neill: the inability to "judge" another person or oneself once the stability of inherited moral law decays into the chaos of individualism.

Maggie survives, but Quentin survives blighted with the knowledge that he, like every man, harbours the desire to kill and the desire to "cure" or save, the equal parts of egomania. It seems unlikely that Holga's minimal hope could rescue him from such a crushing belief.

This nihilistic despair controls the belief and emotion of Miller's most recent play, *Incident at Vichy*. Quentin was shown moving from 1940's Communism to 1960's despair, rather as Miller moved from the simplifying social structure of *All My Sons* to the belief in the hopelessness of human nature itself: "the wish to kill is never killed, but with some gift of courage one may look into its face when it appears, and with a stroke of love—as to an idiot in the house—forgive it; again and again . . . forever?" The climax of *Incident at Vichy* is an act of courage and love within the context of nihilism.

It is a short play, an hour and three quarters in a "place of detention" where nine men and a boy, picked off the streets as suspected Jews, ask themselves about their lives while awaiting interrogation and humiliation for some irrational purpose at the hands of "experts." The stage directions again try to universalize the local action into a representation of western attitudes in the post-war period—no less. Miller's treatment of the Occupation is too broad to be taken seriously, but, once again, as an American play with a European setting for its ideas, it is interesting. On the Left is Bayard, a Communist electrician, the artisan revolutionary, rather in the 1920's Russian film manner. Through him, Miller casts a nostalgic glance at his "felt knowledge" ideology, but while he does allow that ideology may sustain courage, he condescends atrociously to Bayard. For the Communist worker, the meaning of suffering is not personal but historical, a matter of "the economic and political forces" and of "faith in the future; and the future is Socialist." He believes a "viewpoint" sustains a man under violent interrogation because he feels his symbolic nature as a resister against Big Business. His "spirit" is the future.

Miller's treatment of this serious and far from uncommon position is a mockery that can comfort his Broadway audience and let them think that it need not be taken as a criticism of themselves. Next, he offers an artist's stance that only God knows what things "mean"; a business man's confidence that he will be released (he is, and Miller is not interested in whether he is a Jew or not); and an aristocrat's belief that Nazism is not an ideology but "an outburst of vulgarity" to which "many cultivated people" succumbed—why, is not discussed. Monceau, the actor, believes that one plays a role to suit the circumstances. These are responses to the theme of victimization. The actor says, if you don't look like a victim and don't feel like one, you will escape; by "creating one's own reality in this world," you win. If you feel valuable you can create the illusion that "you are who your papers say you are." Thus "they" are defeated. These almost parodistical versions of Miller's obsessive themes are not discussed or acted out, although Leduc, the army psychiatrist, admires the truth of role-playing and the courage to act it through. But to Monceau it is not courage but talent. Miller appears unaware that this kind of pseudo-philosophizing is an effrontery to millions who *were* victimized through Hitler's consciously planned ideological action. For reality he substitutes Bayard's role-playing as worker and Monceau's role-playing as victim. Across this polarity he places the aristocratic Von Berg's argument that a worker can be "confused" into being a Nazi and that only "a few individuals" can resist adoring Hitler—though what this "individual" ability is, is not discussed.

"They," in fact, reduce a man to his nose, his papers and his penis in Vichy, and to the "furnaces" in Poland, and these facts terrorize Leduc into contemplating a plan of escape, like Proctor before him. (Incidentally, woman are not active in *Incident at Vichy*, only present as shadowy irritants behind the scenes.) Von Berg is the centre of Miller's argument that claims the "furnaces" are believable simply because they are "so inconceivably vile." "They" have the power to do the inconceivable: "it paralyzes the rest of us." But what "inconceivable" means is not discussed: all we get is "they are poets, they are striving for a new nobility of the totally vulgar . . . Their motives are musical, and people are merely sounds they play." Moreover, this is the pattern of "the future." The dramatic effect of this speech is seriously to modify the effect of Von Berg's final gesture of love and courage until it becomes absurd as well as sacrificial. This is reinforced by the dialogue between the German major and the Professor from the Race Institute which exposes the irrationality of the penis test, since some Gentiles would not pass it. But the major is trapped by his position into carrying out these tests based on racial absurdity. This situation is in turn backed by Monceau's refusal to believe that his old German audiences could burn actors, while Von Berg tells how a fine young oboe player was arrested only after the police had listened to his rehearsal playing. Leduc challenges Monceau's idea of "creating yourself" when "they point to that spot between your legs." Everything and everybody breaks in the power situation.

Gradually, Von Berg moves into the play's centre. He opposes Monceau's idea that race is a law of the human condition that has simply to be lived with; as Leduc observes accurately, in that case "your heart is conquered territory." But Leduc himself now breaks, Viennese psychology or not. In a dialogue with his fellow war veteran, the major, the psychologist challenges the German officer to prove his claim to be "different" by releasing them: "I will love you as long as I live." But for the German "nothing of that kind is left" and Miller cunningly allows him to support the earlier arguments of Von Berg and Monceau:

> There are no persons any more, don't you see that? There will never be persons again. What do I care if you love me? Are you out of your mind? What am I, a dog that I must be loved? You—*turning to all of them*—goddamned Jews!

Miller has by now equated the despairs of the major, Von Berg and Monceau, got rid of his Communist and his capitalist, and left Leduc with his own absurdity of rejected love. Everything is finally, therefore, a game of power with ciphers. To the major's question "why are you better than anybody else?" Leduc, like Quention, has no reply, since in his terror he admitted that he would accept being released apart from his fellow prisoners. This checkmate of valuelessness enables Miller to dispose of every quality except ultimate selfishness, silence and the shot of a revolver: "I have you at the end of this revolver," the major tells Leduc, "he has me" (indicating the Professor) "—and somebody has somebody else." Miller is playing with the trap or prison situation which haunts American writers in this century, the existential absolute of power control. But he is determined to go on from there. Von Berg and Leduc are left at last with the Old Jew and a vision of endless pointless suffering, repeated meaninglessness, "total, absolute," unsharable waste, on their minds. Even Von Berg had discovered that the weight of his friends' murder or apathy was "seductive"; he had come near to experiencing the sexuality of power (Miller comes no nearer)—"I had dreams at night—Hitler in a great flowing cloak, almost like a gown, almost like a woman. He was beautiful." This total impasse is "the price of idealism"—surely, the most cynical remark that can be made about the twentieth century, even if it is currently fashionable in America.

Von Berg wants ideals he cannot imagine; meanwhile, like Quentin, he has nothing, and it is symbolized by the pathetic bundle of white feathers the Old Jew lets fall as he goes to his interrogation. Miller leaves Von Berg and Leduc in a relationship of cynicism and despair, but without the philosophical and literary details of the final confrontation in *The Representative*. Leduc believes every Gentile is anti-semitic; the Gentile Von Berg refuses to agree. The guilt of Quentin at being relieved of responsibility and love by the death of friends and relations, reappears here in Leduc's definition of "Jew": "the man whose death leaves you relieved that you are not him." In this way Miller reduces the murder of three million Jews, for a particular reason and under particular circumstances, to a bit of philosophical reaction so dogmatic as to rebuff understanding. He makes half-concealed references to Ivan Karamazov and Sartre but cannot rise above mere assertion and counter-assertion in abstraction. The psychologist can only see a future in which men will accept their irrational, murderous nature and understand that their ideals are "only the little tax they pay for the right to hate and kill with a clear conscience." Von Berg counters this abject cynicism only with another assertion: there are still "foolish people and ineffectual" with traditional moral standards. Leduc, like Quentin, believes change will come only when "you face your own complicity" in killer-humanity. Von Berg denies this. And so on.

Out of such a contrived impasse only a sensational gesture could be dramatically tolerable. Miller can suggest no argument for the future based on social change, through economic legislation, education and sexual understanding. Von Berg's thought of suicide if Leduc is right—that Nazis "in some small and frightful part" are doing his will—is irrelevant, and the answer to the question (which Quentin also asks at the end of *After the Fall*) "what can ever save us?" is not another attempt to live (there are no Holgas possible in this play), but personal sacrifice of life, a kind of suicide for another man's life, a martyrdom. Leduc takes his pass to freedom from Von Berg, "his eyes wide in awe and terror." Although there is not, and could not be within the frame of dramatic reference, any discussion of this act of transcendence, what follows renders it an absurd gesture to avoid the impasse of power and meaninglessness. Von Berg and the major stand "forever incomprehensible to one another" and four new prisoners are brought in.

The act of pure sacrifice takes place, therefore, in a vacuum of despair reached through a nihilistic argument based on a false dramatization of a polarity between individualism and idealism. Miller can only see the present repeated endlessly as the future. His nerve has failed, and it is due to his mistaken beliefs. Of *After the Fall* he said it concerned "the human animal's unwillingness or inability to discover in himself the seeds of his own destruction." Life is only possible after "the recognition of the individual's part in the evil he sees and abhors." How the transition, through the self's transformation to some new condition, is to be managed, we are not told. Miller holds to his belief in self-converted individualism rather than the interaction of personal and social change at many levels and in many different ways. The realization that one is involved in a killer-humanity may, after all, encourage one to kill without the burden of guilt. Miller is caught between a belief in a fixed "human nature" and a desire to see it change. His anguish is distressing and devitalizing in its futility. The majority of the world strives forward for peaceful freedom from power situations and their dehumanizing violence, whether in peace or war. Miller, with honesty and persistence, and a degree of dramatic skill, remains fixed in a hell which he maintains cannot be outdated.

Miller repeatedly refers to his dramatic aims as "a balanced concept of life," but fails to find the philosophy and the form to embody this apparently necessary goal. In "The Family in Modern Drama" (1956) he asked a characteristically American question (the tradition is discussed in Harry Levin's *The Power of Blackness*, for example), which he related to a universal and timeless need reflected in the world's drama: "How may a man make of the outside world a home?" He believed this infers a timeless conflict between the individual and the world beyond him, which is the essential dramatic conflict from *Prometheus Bound* to Kaiser's *Gas* and O'Neill's *The Hairy Ape*. The dramatist's "mission" is to formulate this question:

> It is the everlastingly sought balance between order and the need of our souls for freedom; the relatedness between our vaguest longings, our inner questions, and private lives and the life of the generality of men which is our society and our world.

Again, at the conclusion to his introduction to the *Collected Plays* (1957), he stressed a balance which "embraces both determinism and the paradox of will," towards which his plays work as to an "unseen goal." But the terms of this mission themselves destroy the hope of reaching balance: self and society are placed obstinately apart by the very set-up of the actions. Miller's obsessions with "good name," law and authority, self and society, the Unpardonable Sin and the inevitability of suicide in extreme situations, overwhelm his arguments into simplified analyses, confusions and a final paralysis of desperate warnings. Perhaps the release from such an armour can come only from a more detailed understanding of that "little tax" which is the mainspring of trust in human ability to learn and change.

Strength and Weakness in Arthur Miller

by Tom F. Driver

Arthur Miller's introduction to his *Collected Plays* (New York, 1957) is one of the major documents of American theatre. It reveals an eminent playwright having struggled to understand and perfect his craft. It shows him eager to use the theatre to express his evolving ideas. It shows his strengths, and also his weaknesses.

The foremost asset Arthur Miller possesses as a playwright is his knowledge that the theatre must dedicate itself to public matters. He has an acute sense of his audience as persons to be addressed, never merely spectators to be tolerated. "A play," he writes, "ought to make sense to common-sense people . . . the only challenge worth the effort is the widest one and the tallest one, which is the people themselves."

His writing, although it usually has an axe to grind, does not attempt to startle society with new ideas. Indeed, he does not believe that the theatre *can* promulgate entirely new ideas, because it must gather the assent of its audience as it moves along, and this is impossible with the radically new. The theatre should enunciate "not-yet-popular ideas which are already in the air, ideas for which there has already been a preparation by non-dramatic media." Thus he understands the vigor of theatrical art to depend in part on its timeliness: drama is "the art of the present tense par excellence." It follows that the theatre binds isolated human beings into their essential corporateness: "I regard the theatre as a serious business, one that makes or should make man more human, which is to say, less alone."

A corollary of this "public" view of theatre is the belief that psychology is an insufficient basis for it. Psychology becomes preoccupied with the individual, in many cases even the idiosyncratic, whereas the proper concerns of the theatre are social. Miller says that he himself has "shown

"Strength and Weakness in Arthur Miller" by Tom F. Driver. From *Tulane Drama Review*, IV, No. 4 (1960), 45–52. Copyright © 1960 by *Tulane Drama Review*. Reprinted by permission of Tom F. Driver.

a preference for plays which seek causation not only in psychology but in society."

If one takes the "public" view of theatre seriously, he will be forced to ponder the nature of dramatic action and, with it, the importance of the handling of time in the structuring of a play. It has often been said that the problem of dramatic construction is the problem of handling exposition, a truism Miller repeats when he writes, in discussing Ibsen, that "the biggest single dramatic problem" is "how to dramatize what has gone before." It is something other than a truism, however, when he adds:

> I say this not merely out of technical interest, but because dramatic characters, and the drama itself, can never hope to attain a maximum degree of consciousness unless they contain a viable unveiling of the contrast between past and present, and an awareness of the process by which the present has become what it is.

Miller rightly perceives that one of Ibsen's greatest strengths lay in his ability to manage theatrical time so as to express the sequence of causation which he saw in the lives of the characters in his plays. Miller also sees that re-arrangement of time-sequences is tantamount to a change in the implied causal relationships between events. It was just because the notion of causation was so different in *All My Sons* from what it came to be in *Death of a Salesman* that the former remained an "old fashioned" play of exposition, confrontation, and climax, whereas the latter involved "an explosion of watch and calendar," with a corresponding change in the level of reality to which it appealed.

It is hardly possible to read Miller without being impressed with his desire to see and report life realistically. He tells us that when he was writing *A Memory of Two Mondays,* he desired "to be abrupt, clear, and explicit in setting forth fact as fact and art as art so that the sea of theatrical sentiment, which is so easily let in to drown all shape, meaning, and perspective, might be held back and some hard outline of a human dilemma be allowed to rise and stand." Even though there is melodrama in *All My Sons, The Crucible,* and *A View from the Bridge,* it is difficult to reflect on Miller's work without feeling that a hard realism is informing most, if not all, of his concrete observations.

It is the more to his credit as a thinker that his notion of the real is not limited by the canons of what has come to be known in the theatre as "realism." He is quite aware that multiple meanings are attached to the word "real," and while his bent of mind seems to prevent him from investigating the concept of "the real" philosophically, he is far from assuming that the only reality is the positive concrete:

> The longer I dwelt on the whole spectacle, [human dedication to evil] the more clear became the failure of the present age to find a universal moral sanction, and the power of realism's hold on our theatre was an aspect of this vacuum. For it began to appear that our inability to break more than the surfaces of realism reflected our inability—playwrights and audiences— to agree upon the pantheon of forces and values which must lie behind the realistic surfaces of life. In this light, realism, as a style, could seem to be a defense against the assertion of meaning. How strange a conclusion this is when one realizes that the same style seventy years ago was the prime instrument of those who sought to illuminate meaning in the theatre. . . .

Miller describes the way his research into the Salem witch trials led him to understand the limited frame of reference in which modern realistic discourse must be carried on. Out of this came his subsequent attempt to go beyond the limitations of realistic theatre. It is an enlightening tale of a pragmatic mind's discovery of the usefulness of religious language.

What Miller asks for is a theatre of "heightened consciousness." He speaks of two passions in man, the "passion to feel" and the "passion to know." It is his conviction that we need, and can have, more of the latter. "Drama is akin to the other inventions of man in that it ought to help us to know more, and not merely to spend our feelings." The experience of writing *The Crucible* seems to have shown him that a theatre given more to objective knowledge, to heightened self-awareness, is possible. He mentions Brecht as one who has tackled the central problem of contemporary drama, "which is again the problem of consciousness." And in speaking of *Death of a Salesman,* he has the courage to mention its chief limitation when he asks, "but was there not another realm even higher, where feeling took awareness more openly by the hand and both equally ruled and were illuminated?"

These, then, are the strengths of Arthur Miller: an acute awareness of the "public" nature of theatre, the desire to see and report life realistically, an unwillingness to settle for a merely positivist version of reality, and a desire to see a theatre of "heightened consciousness." By putting these concerns before the public, Arthur Miller has shown that his sights are higher than those of any of his competitors at the Broadway box-office. The fact that such concerns exist in a playwright of his prominence is proof that our theatre is still alive.

It is perhaps unfair to judge Miller's work as a playwright by his own critical standard. To do so, however, will reveal not only the deficiencies of much American theatre but will also be a way of seeing certain weaknesses that lie in Miller's thought.

We must remember that the only success both popular and critical Miller has had in this country is *Death of a Salesman*. We must also remember that it remains more consistently upon the level of psychology and feeling than do any of his other plays. The original title for it was *The Inside of His Head,* and the objective, apparently, was to create a dramatic form which "would literally be the process of Willy Loman's way of mind." The result was the kind of play, says Miller, which "issues in a genuine poetry of feeling," and in which feeling is "raised up as the highest good and the ultimate attainment in drama."

It was beyond this level that he wished to go in achieving that other realm, "where feeling took awareness more openly by the hand." Yet when he attempted that other realm in *The Crucible* and *A View from the Bridge,* he was not successful. After *A View from the Bridge* failed in New York, it was revised and later played successfully in London; but it is instructive to note that the revisions were all in the direction of making the psychology of the central character more prominent. Indeed, it had been obvious all along that, although the author of *A View from the Bridge* had wanted to write a play in which action took precedence over psychology, he had chosen for this purpose a character and situation bound to interest the audience primarily from a psychological point of view. It was the story of a Brooklyn longshoreman unconsciously in love with his niece, a man who destroys all his family because of jealousy.

In classical times, such a theme might have served a trans-psychological purpose; but in Miller's play there was no level of meaning, law, providence, or fate, upon which an action that transcended character might rest. The action inevitably fell back, as it were, into the subjectivity of Eddie and his uncontrollable jealousy. No genuine parallel with the Greek drama had been found. In the case of Oedipus, for instance, the objective realm is clearly expressed in the problem of the health of the Theban *polis,* the proscriptions against patricide and incest, and the search for truth as a self-evident good. Nothing on this level was present in *A View from the Bridge,* yet without it no theatre of action rather than character is possible. Mr. Miller had not, in short, solved the problem of "the failure of the present age to find a universal moral sanction," and without such a solution, in one degree or another, there was nothing other than psychology to support the action of his play.

From this experience Mr. Walter Kerr would doubtless argue, as he does in *How Not to Write a Play,* that it is only psychological consistency and the creation of interesting character which makes good plays, and that the one undoubted success of Arthur Miller, *Death of a Salesman,* shows it. All that it really shows, however, is that Arthur Miller is typical of our theatre in being able to do character best and in not being able to sustain a more comprehensive kind of action.

Two weaknesses are fatal to Miller's attempt to write the kind of objective theatre he sees is needed. First, his view of man in society is too narrow. He is restricted, as many have pointed out, by a particular social theory which he seems not to have had the inclination to probe until it yielded him a fundamental idea of human nature. Brecht, to take an opposite example, did such probing. Apparently Miller's Marxism changes as he goes along, and it would be going beyond the evidence to suggest that he adheres to any "line," whether political or ideological. Nevertheless, he bears a quasi-Marxist stamp and most of his plays tend to become mere partisan social critique. The momentary usefulness of that social critique, or the extent to which it actually is Marxist, is nothing to the point. The point is simply that his conception of the "reality" with which man must deal is limited.

Miller has some lofty things to say about *All My Sons* being an attack upon "unrelatedness" and about crime "having roots in a certain relationship of the individual to society;" but when all is said and done, the play seems to be only a play about an aircraft-parts manufacturer in wartime. It has rapidly become dated. The mistake was not in being timely, but in being timely with too simple a point of view. *The Crucible* invited the immediate application to the McCarthy issue which it received, and which made it seem small. When it was revived in 1958 off Broadway, it did have more success than in its first run during the McCarthy era. Even then, however, I found the play strident, written with an emotion inappropriate to its inner life.

> Our drama is condemned, so to speak, to the emotions of subjectivism, which, as they approach knowledge and self-awareness, become less and less actual and real to us. In retrospect, I think that my course in *The Crucible* should have been toward greater self-awareness and not, as my critics have implied, toward an enlarged and more pervasive subjectivism.

The goal is right. It is not reached because Miller's sense of objectivity is not comprehensive enough. He lacks that metaphysical inquisitiveness which would take him to the bottom of the problems he encounters. One might say that he sees the issues too soon, sees them in their preliminary form of social or even moral debate, but not in terms of dramatic events that disturb the audience's idea of basic truth, which is the foundation for its moral attitudes. It is the genius of a Pirandello, a Brecht, or an Ionesco to cause such disturbance and by doing so to become genuine moral critics. Miller's limited theatre fits down inside the theatre of the world which the audience inhabits. His theatre is too small to touch the outer walls against which the genuinely objective drama would need to be played.

This point is made very clear in certain remarks he makes about *Death of a Salesman,* especially as we compare them with the confusion which lurks in every corner of that play. The following passage occurs in a discussion of Willy Loman's stature as a tragic figure:

> How can we respect a man who goes to such extremities over something he could in no way help or prevent? The answer, I think, is not that we respect the man, but that we respect the Law he has so completely broken, wittingly or not, for it is that Law which, we believe, defines us as men. The confusion of some critics viewing *Death of a Salesman* in this regard is that they do not see that Willy Loman has broken a law without whose protection life is insupportable if not incomprehensible to him and to many others; it is the law which says that a failure in society and in business has no right to live. Unlike the law against incest, the law of success is not administered by statute or church, but it is very nearly as powerful in its grip upon men. The confusion increases because, while it is a law, it is by no means a wholly agreeable one even as it is slavishly obeyed, for to fail is no longer to belong to society, in his estimate.

The confusion, I am afraid, lies not with the critics but with the playwright, and it is a very illustrative one. There is, in fact, no "law which says that a failure in society and in business has no right to live." It would, indeed, suit Miller's polemic better if there were. There is a *delusion* that a failure in society and in business has no right to live. To some people, such as Willy Loman, it may indeed seem like a law. But it is one thing for a character in a play to act as if something were a law, and quite another thing for the playwright to believe it. Miller's subsequent remarks in this same section of his essay make it perfectly clear that he himself, the audience, and also Willy Loman, do as a matter of fact have criteria according to which they suspect that this "law" is a hoax. It is in fact not a law but a false *credo,* which Willy shares with many persons, and the result of the attempt to make a false *credo* into a law results only in pathetic irony.

What is it, one wonders, that prevents Miller from probing Willy's consciousness and ours to the point of finding the truly objective world in which we still, in fact, believe and according to which Willy's "law" strikes us as so pathetic? If we ask where in the play one touches bed-rock, the answer is nowhere. Is the law of success *really* a law? No. Miller tells us that "the system of love," which is "embodied in Biff Loman," was meant to counter Willy's "law." But if that is true, it was unfortunately not dramatized. That is, the way in which Biff's "law" of love judges and invalidates Willy's "law" of success is not revealed, and so the one is not actually a truth which is being brought to bear dramatically on the other.

The same ambiguity is seen in the question of society versus the individual. John Gassner said long ago that Arthur Miller had "split his play between *social causation* and *individual responsibility* for Willy's fate." [1] Is Willy's "law" the result of some defect in himself? If so, what is the nature of this defect, and what genuine law does it confound? Or is his "law" imposed upon him by a white-collar industrial society? If so, what is wrong with such a society and what truths does it prevent Willy Loman from seeing? Miller would probably resist making a decision in favor of either the individual or the social causation, and rightly so. But in that case, if he is interested in theatre worth the name of art, he has an obligation to examine his complex situation until the roots of Willy's anxiety are exposed, an exposure which would cause us to know something about the reality in which we are, if only unconsciously, living. It is in the lack of penetration into the objective philosophical situation that Miller fails us, with the result that we must settle for no more enlightenment upon our situation than pathetic Willy had upon his.

Miller deplores the loss of a "universal moral sanction," but he does nothing toward the discovery of a conceivable basis for one. In that respect he is, perhaps, no different from the majority of his contemporaries. It is not a surprising result, however, that he falls so easily into preaching and scolding his audience. (In his essay in the *Collected Plays* he is not above reproving those who staged or acted his plays, an attitude which reflects credit upon no one, least of all the playwright.) Miller's

[1] John Gassner, *The Theatre in Our Times,* New York, 1954, p. 347. Author's italics.

strident moralism is a good example of what happens when ideals must be maintained in an atmosphere of humanistic relativism. There being no objective good and evil, and no imperative other than conscience, man himself must be made to bear the full burden of creating his values and living up to them. The immensity of this task is beyond human capacity, even that of genius. To insist upon it without reference to ultimate truth is to create a situation productive of despair. This point has been seen by many writers of our day, but not by the liberal optimists, of which Miller is one. Here we have come to the second weakness which inevitably robs his work of stature.

At the time that *The Crucible* opened, Eric Bentley categorized Arthur Miller as an unreconstructed liberal and said that he "is the playwright of American liberal folklore." [2] The trouble with the play, he went on, was that it too neatly divided the sheep from the goats. "The guilty men are as black with guilt as Mr. Miller says—what we must ask is whether the innocent are as white with innocence." Mr. Bentley's remarks become all the more interesting when they are remembered in connection with a passage in the introduction to the *Collected Plays,* in which Miller describes his discovery, while writing *The Crucible,* of certain facts about human nature:

> I believe now, as I did not conceive then, that there are people dedicated to evil in the world; that without their perverse example we should not know the good. Evil is not a mistake but a fact in itself . . . I believe merely that, from whatever cause, a dedication to evil, not mistaking it for good, but knowing it as evil and loving it as evil, is possible in human beings who appear agreeable and normal. I think now that one of the hidden weaknesses of our whole approach to dramatic psychology is our inability to face this fact—to conceive, in effect, of Iago.

So far, we are on fairly safe ground, although we must note already that only certain people are dedicated to evil, others presumably going clean. But note how contradictory are the following sentiments. They are from the very same passage, in the place indicated above by the ellipsis:

> I have never proceeded psychoanalytically in my thought, but neither have I been separated from that humane if not humanistic conception of man as being essentially innocent while the evil in him represents but a perversion of his frustrated love. I posit no metaphysical force of evil which totally

[2] Eric Bentley, *The Dramatic Event,* New York, 1954, p. 92.

possesses certain individuals, nor do I even deny that given infinite wisdom and patience and knowledge any human being can be saved from himself.

Here the contradictory and self-limiting sentiments pass clearly before us. Evil is a fact, yet it is only a perversion of frustrated love. It is as absolute as in Iago, yet it may be cured with wisdom, patience, and knowledge. It is outside one's self and may be loved, yet it is only from himself that man needs to be saved. The passage reveals a head-on collision between illusions of human goodness and the facts of dedication to evil. Here we reach the straits through which the Miller realism will not pass.

No wonder *Death of a Salesman* cannot make up its mind whether the trouble is in Willy or in society. No wonder Willy is at one moment the pathetic object of our pity and the next is being defended as a hero of tragic dimensions. Miller is a playwright who wants morality without bothering to speak of a good in the light of which morality would make sense. On the one hand he wants a universal moral sanction; on the other he considers man's potentialities and limitations to lie entirely within himself. Out of such unresolved contradictions irony and pathos are the most we can get, and we are lucky to get those.

The concluding sentence of the essay we have been considering reads as follows:

> If there is one unseen goal toward which every play in this book strives, it is that very discovery and its proof—that we are made and yet are more than what made us.

I take this to mean that man transcends his hereditary and environmental situation. Well and good. But if we are to be able to speak of "moral sanctions" in drama or society, we must come to acknowledge that man is himself transcended by some truth that is not irrelevant to morality. Miller seems to flinch before that assertive act of the imagination which uncovers (or, in religious language, receives) the ontological ground upon which the truly meaningful act must stand. This is a level of the real which Miller has not yet explored, although it is the level demanded of one who would break out of the confusions that enveloped Willy Loman.

The Realism of Arthur Miller

by Raymond Williams

I

The most important single fact about the plays of Arthur Miller is that he has brought back into the theatre, in an important way, the drama of social questions. It has been fashionable, certainly in England, to reject such drama as necessarily superficial. In part, this rejection is in itself social, for it has shown itself in the context of a particular phase of consciousness: that widespread withdrawal from social thinking which came to its peak in the late nineteen-forties, at just the time when we were first getting to know Arthur Miller as a dramatist. Yet the rejection can be seen, also, as critically necessary, for there is little doubt that the dramatic forms in which social questions were ordinarily raised had become, in general, inadequate: a declined, low-pressure naturalism, or else the angularity of the self-conscious problem play, the knowingness of the post-expressionist social revue. To break out from this deadlock needed three things, in any order: a critical perception of why the forms were inadequate; effective particular experiment; a revival, at depth and with passion, of the social thinking itself. Arthur Miller is unquestionably the most important agent of this break-out, which as yet, however, is still scattered and uncertain. His five plays to date show a wide and fascinating range of experiment, and the introduction he has written to the collected edition of them shows an exceptionally involved and perceptive critical mind, both self-conscious and self-critical of the directions of his creative effort. Yet, while he could not have written his plays without these qualities, it is probably true that the decisive factor, in his whole achievement, is a particular kind and intensity of social thinking, which in his case seems both to underlie and to determine the critical scrutiny

"The Realism of Arthur Miller" by Raymond Williams. From *Critical Quarterly*, I (Summer, 1959), 140–49. Reprinted by permission of Raymond Williams and Chatto & Windus Ltd.

and the restless experimentation. In seeking to define the magnificent realism of the great tradition of nineteenth-century fiction, I wrote of that kind of work which "seeks to create and judge the quality of a whole way of life in terms of the qualities of persons":[1]

> Neither element, neither the society nor the individual, is there as a priority. The society is not a background against which the personal relationships are studied, nor are the individuals merely illustrations of aspects of the way of life. Every aspect of personal life is radically affected by the quality of the general life, yet the general life is seen at its most important in completely personal terms.

I argued that this "social" tradition had broken down, in fiction, into the separate forms of the "personal" and the "sociological," and I would make the same analysis, with certain changes of detail, in the case of twentieth-century drama. The key to social realism, in these terms, lies in a particular conception of the relationship of the individual to society, in which neither is the individual seen as a unit nor the society as an aggregate, but both are seen as belonging to a continuous and in real terms inseparable process. My interest in the work of Arthur Miller is that he seems to have come nearer than any other post-war writer (with the possible exceptions of Albert Camus and Albrecht Goes) to this substantial conception. Looking at it from one point of view, he has restored active social criticism to the drama, and has written on such contemporary themes as the social accountability of business, the forms of the success-ethic, intolerance and thought-control, the nature of modern work-relations. Yet he has written "about" these in such a way as to distinguish his work quite clearly from the ordinary sociological problem-play, for at his best he has seen these problems as living tissue, and his most successful characters are not merely "aspects of the way of life," but individuals who are ends and values in themselves:

> He's a human being, and a terrible thing is happening to him. So attention must be paid . . . Attention, attention must be finally paid to such a person.

It is from this centre—a new or newly-recovered way of social thinking, which is also powerfully available as direct experience—that any estimate of Arthur Miller as a dramatist must begin.

[1] See Raymond Williams, "Realism and the Contemporary Novel," *Partisan Review,* XXVI (Spring, 1959), 200–213.

II

Miller's first two published plays[2]—he had written seven or eight others before this success—are *All My Sons* (1947) and *Death of a Salesman* (1949). It is extremely interesting to compare these two, because while they are very different in method they are also quite obviously very deeply linked, in experience. *All My Sons* has been described as an Ibsenite play, and certainly, if we restrict Ibsen to the kind of play he wrote between *The League of Youth* (1869) and *Rosmersholm* (1886), it is a relevant description. The similarities are indeed so striking that we could call *All My Sons* pastiche if the force of its conception were not so evident. It is perhaps that much rarer case, of a writer who temporarily discovers in an existing form an exact way of realising his own experience. At the center of the play is the kind of situation which was Ibsen's development of the device of the "fatal secret." Joe Keller, a small manufacturer, has (in a similar way to Consul Bernick in *Pillars of Society*) committed a social crime for which he has escaped responsibility. He acquiesced in the sending of defective parts to the American Air Force in wartime, and yet allowed another man to take the consequences and imprisonment. The action begins after the war, and is basically on the lines of what has been called Ibsen's retrospective method (it was always much more than a device of exposition; it is a thematic forcing of past into present). The Ibsen method of showing first an ordinary domestic scene, into which, by gradual infiltration, the crime and the guilt enter and build up to the critical eruption, is exactly followed. The process of this destructive infiltration is carefully worked out in terms of the needs of the other characters—Keller's wife and surviving son, the girl the son is to marry, the neighbours, the son of the convict—so that the demonstration of social consequence, and therefore of Keller's guilt, is not in terms of any abstract principle, but in terms of personal needs and relationships, which compose a reality that directly enforces the truth. If Keller's son had not wanted to marry the convicted man's daughter (and they had been childhood friends; it was that neighbourhood which Keller's act disrupted); if his wife, partly in reaction to her knowledge

[2] There were earlier published plays, but none obviously that Miller cared to put into *Collected Plays*.

of his guilt, had not maintained the superstition that their son killed in the war was still alive; if the action had been between strangers or business acquaintances, rather than between neighbours and neighbouring families, the truth would never have come out. Thus we see a true social reality, which includes both social relationships and absolute personal needs, enforcing a social fact—that of responsibility and consequence. This is still the method of Ibsen in the period named, and the device of climax—a concealed letter from Keller's dead son, who had known of his father's guilt—is again directly in Ibsen's terms.

The elements of theatrical contrivance in Ibsen's plays of this kind, and in *All My Sons,* are now sufficiently clear. Yet the total effect of such a play is undoubtedly powerful if its experience truly corresponds to its conventions. In historical terms, this is a bourgeois form, with that curious combination of a demonstrated public morality and an intervening fate, evident in the early 18th century domestic drama, and reaching its maturity in Ibsen. To a considerable extent, *All My Sons* is a successful late example of this form, but a point is reached, in Miller's handling of the experience, where its limits are touched. For, as he rightly sees it, the social reality is more than a mechanism of honesty and right dealing, more than Ibsen's definition—

> The spirits of Truth and Freedom, these are the pillars of society.[3]

Miller reaches out to a deeper conception of relationships, which he emphasises in his title. This is something more than honesty and uprightness: it is the quite different social conception of human brotherhood—

> I think to him they were all my sons. And I guess they were, I guess they were.[4]

Moreover, Miller sees this in a social context, as he explains in the Introduction:

> Joe Keller's trouble . . . is not that he cannot tell right from wrong but that his cast of mind cannot admit that he, personally, has any viable connection with his world, his universe, or his society. He is not a partner in society, but an incorporated member, so to speak, and you cannot sue personally the officers of a corporation. I hasten to make clear that I am not merely speaking of a literal corporation but the concept of a man's becoming

[3] This is Lona Hessel's line in *Pillars of Society,* the last line in the play.
[4] This is the last line Joe Keller speaks before he goes off-stage to shoot himself.

a function of production or distribution to the point where his personality becomes divorced from the actions it propels.[5]

This concept, though Miller does not use the term, is the classical Marxist concept of alienation, and it is with alienation embodied both in a social action and in a personality that Miller is ultimately concerned. The true social reality—the needs and destinies of other persons—is meant to break down this alienated consciousness, and restore the fact of consequence, of significant and continuing relationships, in this man and in his society. But then it is at this point, as I see it, that the limits of the form are damaging. The words I have quoted, expressing Keller's realisation of a different kind of consciousness, have to stand on their own, because unlike the demonstration of ordinary social responsibility they have no action to support them, and moreover as words they are limited to the conversational resources so adequate elsewhere in the play, but wholly inadequate here to express so deep and substantial a personal discovery (and if it is not this it is little more than a maxim, a "sentiment"). It is at this point that we see the naturalist form—even a principled naturalism, as in Ibsen and Miller and so rarely in others; even this substantially and powerfully done—breaking down as it has so often broken down: partly for the reasons I argued in *Drama from Ibsen to Eliot*[6] (the inadequacy of conversational writing in any deep crisis); partly, I would now add, because the consciousness which the form was designed to express is in any serious terms obsolete, and was already, by Miller himself, being reached beyond.

There is an interesting account, in Miller's Introduction, of the genesis of *All My Sons*, relating it to a previous play and the discovery that

> two of the characters, who had been friends in the previous drafts, were logically brothers and had the same father . . . The overt story was only tangential to the secret drama which its author was quite unconsciously trying to write . . . In writing of the father-son relationship and of the son's search for his relatedness there was a fullness of feeling I had never known before. The crux of *All My Sons* was formed; and the roots of *Death of a Salesman* were sprouted.

This is extremely important, not only as a clue to the plays named, but as indicating the way in which Miller, personally, came to the experience

---

[5] This quotation and those on the following pages are from Miller's Introduction to *Collected Plays*.

[6] Raymond Williams, *Drama from Ibsen to Eliot* (London: Chatto & Windus, 1952).

expressible as that of human brotherhood. In any sense that matters, this concept is always personally known and lived; as a slogan it is nothing. And the complicated experience of inheritance from a father is perhaps one of the permanent approaches to this transforming consciousness. There is the creative complexity of the fact that a son, in many senses, replaces his father. There is dependence and the growth to independence, and both are necessary, in a high and moving tension. In both father and son there are the roots of guilt, and yet, ultimately they stand together as men—the father both a model and a rejected ideal; the son both an idea and a relative failure. But the model, the rejection, the idea and the failure are all terms of growth, and the balance that can be struck is a very deep understanding of relatedness and brotherhood. One way of looking at *All My Sons* is in these universal terms: the father, in effect, destroys one of his sons, and that son, in his turn, gives sentence of death on him, while at the same time, to the other son, the father offers a future, and the son, in rejecting it, destroys his father, in pain and love. Similarly, in *Death of a Salesman*, Willy Loman, like Joe Keller, has lived for his sons, will die of the son who was to extend his life, yet the sons, in their different ways, reject him, in one case for good reasons, and in effect destroy him. Yet the failure on both sides is rooted in love and dependence; the death and the love are deeply related aspects of the same relationship. This complex, undoubtedly, is the "secret drama" of which Miller writes, and if it is never wholly expressed it is clearly the real source of the extraordinary dramatic energy.

Death of a Salesman takes the moment of crisis in which Joe Keller could only feebly express himself, and makes of it the action of the whole play. Miller's first image was of

> an enormous face . . . which would appear and then open up, and we would see the inside of a man's head. In fact, *The Inside of His Head* was the first title.

This, in dramatic terms, is expressionism, and correspondingly the guilt of Willy Loman is not in the same world as that of Joe Keller: it is not a single act, subject to public process, needing complicated grouping and plotting to make it emerge; it is, rather, the consciousness of a whole life. Thus the expressionist method, in the final form of the play, is not a casual experiment, but rooted in the experience. It is the drama of a single mind, and moreover, it would be false to a more integrated—or less disintegrating—personality.

It is historically true that expressionism is attuned to the experience of disintegration. In general dramatic history, as in Miller's own development, it arises at that point where the limits of naturalism are touched and a hitherto stable form begins to break to pieces. Yet *Death of a Salesman* is actually a development of expressionism, of an interesting kind. As Miller puts it:

> I had always been attracted and repelled by the brilliance of German expressionism after World War I, and one aim in "Salesman" was to employ its quite marvellous shorthand for humane "felt" characterisations rather than for purposes of demonstration for which the Germans had used it.

This is a fair comment on the "social expressionism" of, say, Toller, and the split of expressionism into "personal" and "social" kinds is related to the general dissociation which I earlier discussed. *Death of a Salesman* is an expressionist reconstruction of naturalist substance, and the result is not hybrid but a powerful particular form. The continuity from social expressionism remains clear, however, for I think in the end it is not Willy Loman as a man, but the image of the Salesman, that predominates. The social figure sums up the theme referred to as alienation, for this is a man who from selling things has passed to selling himself, and has become, in effect, a commodity which like other commodities will at a certain point be economically discarded. The persuasive atmosphere of the play (which the slang embodies so perfectly, for it is a social result of this way of living) is one of false consciousness—the conditioned attitudes in which Loman trains his sons—being broken into by real consciousness, in actual life and relationships. The expressionist method embodies this false consciousness much more powerfully than naturalism could do. In *All My Sons* it had to rest on a particular crime, which could then be seen as in a limiting way personal—Keller the black sheep in a white flock—although the fundamental criticism was of a common way of living and thinking. The "marvellous shorthand" is perfectly adapted to exposing this kind of illusion and failure. At the same time the structure of personal relationships, within this method, must be seen as in a sense arbitrary; it has nothing of the rooted detail which the naturalism of *All My Sons* in this respect achieved. The golden football hero, the giggling woman in the hotel, the rich brother, and similar figures seem to me to be clichés from the thinner world of a work like *Babbitt,* which at times the play uncomfortably resembles.[7] The final figure of a man killing himself for the insurance money caps the whole process of the life that has been demonstrated, but "demonstrated," in spite of Miller's comment on the Germans, is the word that occurs to one to describe it. The emotional power of the demonstration is considerable, and is markedly increased by the brilliant expressionist staging. Yet, by the high standards which Miller insists on, and in terms of the essential realism to which he seems to be reaching, the contrast of success and failure within both *All My Sons* and *Death of a Salesman* points finally to the radical and still unsolved difficulties of form.

III

The Crucible (1952) is a powerful and successful dramatisation of the notorious witch-trials of Salem, but it is technically less interesting than its predecessors just because it is based on a historical event which at the level of action and principled statement is explicit enough to solve, or not to raise, the difficult dramatic problems which Miller had previously set himself. The importance of the witch-trials is that in them, in a clear and exciting way, the moral crisis of a society is explicit, is directly enacted and stated, in such a way that the quality of the whole way of life is organically present and evident in the qualities of persons. Through this action Miller brilliantly expresses a particular crisis—the modern witchhunt—in his own society, but it is not often, in our own world, that the issues and statements so clearly emerge in a naturally dramatic form. The methods explored in the earlier plays are not necessary here, but the problems they offered to solve return immediately, outside the context of this particular historical event. *The Crucible* is a fine play, but it is also a quite special case.

In *A Memory of Two Mondays* (1955), Miller returns to the direct dramatisation of modern living, and as if to underline the point made about *The Crucible* (of which, as the Introduction shows, he was completely aware) seeks to make a new form out of the very facts of inconsequence, discontinuity, and the deep frustrations of inarticulacy, which is at once a failure of speech and the wider inability of men to express

---

[7] For a detailed comparison of "Salesman" with *Babbitt* see Gordon W. Couchman, "Arthur Miller's Tragedy of Babbitt," *Educational Theatre Journal*, VII (October, 1955), 206–11.

themselves in certain kinds of work and working relationship. Instead of concentrating these themes in a particular history, pointed by plot or single crisis, he deploys them in the scattered form of a series of impressions, with the dramatic center in memory rather than in action or crisis. The work atmosphere is in some ways significantly caught, and there is always the mark of Miller's insight into the importance and passion of what many others dismiss as "ordinary" lives. There is an occasional flare of dramatic feeling, as in the last speech of Gus, but in general the tension is much lower than in the earlier plays, and the dramatic methods seem often mere devices. The Irish singer and reciter; the insets of flat sub-Auden verse; the lighting and scenic devices of the passing of time: these, at this tension, seem mechanical. And a central image of the play—when the workers clean the windows to let in a sight of sun and trees, and let in actually a view of a cat-house (brothel)—seems to me contrived. Miller's fertility of experiment is important, but experiment, as here, involves failure.

A View from the Bridge (1955; revised 1957)[8] brings back the intensity. The capacity to touch and stir deep human feeling was marked in the earlier plays, but Miller has said, interestingly (it is his essential difference from Tennessee Williams, with whom he is often linked):

> The end of drama is the creation of a higher consciousness and not merely a subjective attack upon the audience's nerves and feelings.

The material of *A View from the Bridge* is to most people deeply disturbing, and Miller's first impulse was to keep it abstract and distant, to hold back

> the empathic flood which a realistic portrayal of the same tale and characters might unloose.

But, in his own view, he went too far in this direction, and subsequently revised the play towards a more intense realism. The distancing element remains, however, in the use of a commentator, or *raisonneur*, and, though there are false notes in the writing of this part, it is an important reason for the play's success.

A View from the Bridge follows from the earlier works in that it shows a man being broken and destroyed by guilt. Its emphasis is personal, though the crisis is related to the intense primary relationships

---

[8] Although "View" was revised for its London production in October 1956, the revised edition was not published until 1957 in *Collected Plays*.

of an insecure and partly illegal group—a Brooklyn waterfront slum, with ties back to Italy, receiving unauthorised immigrants and hiding them within its own fierce loyalties. Eddie Carbone's breakdown is sexual, and the guilt, as earlier, is deeply related to love. And the personal breakdown leads to a sin against this community, when in the terror of his complicated jealousies Eddie betrays immigrants of his wife's kin to the external law.

At the centre of the drama again is the form of a relationship between parent and child, but here essentially displaced so that the vital relationship is between a man and the niece to whom he has been as a father. The girl's coming to adolescence provokes a crisis which is no more soluble than if they had really been father and child, yet to a degree perhaps is more admissible into consciousness. Eddie is shown being destroyed by forces which he cannot control, and the complex of love and guilt has the effect of literal disintegration, in that the known sexual rhythms break down into their perverse variations: the rejection of his wife, as his vital energy transfers to the girl, and then the shattering crisis in which within the same rush of feeling he moves into the demonstration of both incestuous and homosexual desires. The crisis burns out his directions and meanings, and he provokes his death shouting "I want my name." This establishment of significance, after breakdown, through death, was the pattern of Joe Keller and Willy Loman; of John Proctor, in heroic stance, in *The Crucible*; of Gus, in a minor key, in *A Memory of Two Mondays*. We are at the heart, here, of Miller's dramatic pattern, and his work, in this precise sense, is tragedy—the loss of meaning in life turns to the struggle for meaning by death. The loss of meaning is always a personal history, though in Willy Loman it comes near to being generalized. Equally, it is always set in the context of a loss of social meaning, a loss of meaning in relationships. The point is made, and is ratifying, in the commentary in *A View from the Bridge:*

Now we are quite civilized, quite American. Now we settle for half . . .

and again, at the end:

. . . Something perversely pure calls to me from his memory—not purely good, but himself purely, for he allowed himself to be wholly known and for that I think I will love him more than all my sensible clients. And yet, it is better to settle for half, it must be! And so I mourn him—I admit it—with a certain alarm.

Tempted always to settle for half—for the loss of meaning and the loss of consequence endemic in the whole complex of personal and social relationships, the American way of living as Miller sees it—the heroes of these plays, because, however perversely, they are still attached to life, still moved by irresistible desires for a name, a significance, a vital meaning, break out and destroy themselves, leaving their own comment on the half-life they have experienced. Miller's drama, as he has claimed, is a drama of consciousness, and in reaching out for this new social consciousness—in which "every aspect of personal life is radically affected by the quality of the general life, yet the general life is seen at its most important in completely personal terms"—Miller, for all the marks of difficulty, uncertainty and weakness that stand within the intensity of his effort, seems clearly a central figure in the drama and consciousness of our time.

Arthur Miller and the Idea of Modern Tragedy

by M. W. Steinberg

"Anyone who dares to discuss the making of tragedy," cautions Max-well Anderson, "lays himself open to critical assault and general barrage" —a warning that has not deterred modern scholars, if we are to judge by the many books and articles on the subject. On reading the critical literature on tragedy, one is impressed by the number of widely differ-ing definitions. One finds the assertion, for example, put forward by Joseph Wood Krutch and others, that virtually no modern play is tragic because the protagonist is not of exalted rank. At the other extreme, we find more tolerant critics who are willing to accept as tragedies almost any serious play that must perforce involve conflict and suffering. F. L. Lucas, in his book *Tragedy*, says that if we attempted to remould the Aristotelian definition in the light of the history of tragedy, we would get something like this tautology: "Serious drama is a serious representation by speech and action of some phase of human life." And he adds, "If there is an unhappy ending, we may call it tragedy; but if the play is a serious attempt to represent life, it makes no great differ-ence whether or not good fortune intervenes in the last scene." In many articles during the past ten or eleven years Arthur Miller has attempted to formulate an acceptable modern definition, and an examination of his plays and his essays on tragedy will not only reveal the terms of his definition, but may also indicate something of the relation between modern tragedy and that of earlier periods.

As the twentieth century approached, various forces were making for realism in drama with its emphasis on people and situations drawn from ordinary life. In part this interest reflected the growth of democracy and the extension of education to the masses which introduced the era of the common man. Perhaps an even more important aspect of the

"Arthur Miller and the Idea of Modern Tragedy" by M. W. Steinberg. From *Dal-housie Review*, XL (1960), 329-40. Reprinted by permission of M. W. Steinberg and the *Dalhousie Review*.

new drama was the post-Darwinian emphasis on environment as a shaping force in life. Man was seen as the product, and from one point of view the victim, of his surroundings. Increasingly, writers became preoccupied with social institutions, political and economic issues, and these they presented as best they could objectively, or "scientifically." The primary concern was with the external factors that operated on the protagonist, rather than with the inner crisis experienced by him when challenged by his conditions. In Ibsen's *A Doll House*, for example, the central concern is with the social forces that unfortunately made woman dependent and limited. We are not invited to witness and vicariously participate in a personal tragedy with universal application, but rather we are directly involved and made aware of our guilt, our responsibility for the social milieu that makes for tragedy. A blow is aimed at us; the dramatist uses his characters to compel us to consider a social problem. Shaw, following in this pattern, makes his purpose clear in his Preface to *Plays Unpleasant*. He writes,

> I must, however, warn my readers that my attacks are directed against themselves, not against my stage figures. They cannot too thoroughly understand that the guilt of defective social organization does not lie alone on the people who actually work the commercial makeshifts which the defects make inevitable, and who often, like Sartorius and Mrs. Warren, display valuable executive capacities and even high moral virtues in their administration, but with the whole body of citizens whose public opinion, public action, and public contribution as ratepayers, alone can replace Sartorius's slums with decent dwellings, Charteris's intrigues with reasonable marriage contracts, and Mrs. Warren's profession with honorable industries guarded by a humane industrial code and a 'moral minimum' wage.

This concern with the social problem, the social injustice and its effect on the lives of the characters, is found in Miller's plays too. The economic basis of social mischief is as obvious in *All My Sons* as in Shaw's *Widowers' Houses* or Ibsen's *An Enemy of the People*; in *Death of a Salesman* the common man is crushed by forces outside himself and by illusions, false ideals, spawned by those forces; and in *The Crucible* the political motif is clear. Miller refused to regard this emphasis as in any way negating the high seriousness of his plays or diminishing their tragic quality.

On the other hand, it is sometimes charged that such plays are not really tragic because they rub our noses in the social mire and depress rather than exalt; because they end with a stated or implied call to action rather than with a feeling of catharsis, a sense of "all passion spent"; or because they conclude with a note of question rather than with a sense of our being reconciled to life. According to such a view, the tragic hero through his struggle and the recognition of his own short-coming reveals man's essential or potential nobility, and we are ennobled, uplifted by the spectacle. While this view undoubtedly holds true for some of the finest tragedies ever written, we may not only doubt its comprehensiveness but even question its application to plays that are unquestionably accepted by these same critics as tragedies. Are we, for example, reconciled to the death of Othello or uplifted by it? Here is a good man whose goodness has been imposed upon. Though he recognizes his error, there is no evidence of amendment or opportunity for it. He has already killed Desdemona, so any effective amendment in that direction is obviously impossible. His suicide indicates that he accepts his guilt, but certainly the compounding of corpses cannot reconcile us to the tragic situation. While it is true that the action brings out a flaw in Othello's character, it is not of such a nature that it merits his death: the punishment does not fit the crime or, rather, weakness. Our sense of justice is shocked—or ought to be; we are morally offended at the disparity between what we consider just and what "fate" metes out. Furthermore, even if we accept Othello's death as just, what about the death of Desdemona, the innocent? What about the death of Cordelia, of Duncan, of Lady Macduff and her children? The superb poetry at the end of *Hamlet* and *Lear,* which diverts us and cushions the shock of the horrors revealed, does not really change the fact that this is a world in which Hamlet is treacherously poisoned and Cordelia is found hanging. On what basis can we be reconciled to such a scheme of things? Within the terms of our earthly existence, only by confirmed pessimism, bitter or passive stoicism, and a kind of grim satisfaction—or a sense of exaltation if we are romantics—at our capacity for struggle and endurance. But even where such a sense of exaltation or reconciliation existed in the traditional tragedy, it could be achieved only by focussing on the hero and ignoring the world in which he moved, for in that world there is injustice and unmerited suffering—unless one postulated a God or gods whose ways, though incomprehensible to us morally, were accepted as just. This kind of reconciliation the modern dramatist, with the exception perhaps of T. S. Eliot, is unwilling to accept. But, at the same time, he is not willing to accept the initial situation, that of man in a sorry world, as fixed and final. He makes no

clear distinction between the order of things and man in the order. For
him there is a continuing inter-relationship, a possibility of development.
The dramatist, as Arthur Miller insists, must not conceive of man as a
private entity and his social relations as something thrown at him, but
rather he must come to see that "society is inside of man and man is
inside society, and you cannot even create a truthfully drawn psychological entity on the stage until you understand his social relations and
their power to make him what he is and to prevent him from being
what he is not." Man is seen as constantly in the process of becoming,
shaped and not merely stimulated by his environment, his fate. But
there is nothing fixed about his fate—it too is subject to change; it has
no eternal metaphysical basis. Tragedy, says Miller, must question everything; from the total questioning we learn. Hence the onslaught on
social conditions in post-Ibsen drama and the optimistic premise underlying the tragedy: earth and high heaven do not ail from the prime
foundation, and the troubles that beset us are not visited on us from on
high by mysterious or vengeful deities. Implied is the social reformer's
call to take up arms against our troubles, and his confidence that we can
by opposing end them. The possibility of a way to the better, however,
does not alter the fact that the full look at the worst, at the moment,
reveals tragedy.

In one of his earliest essays on drama, "Tragedy and the Common
Man," Arthur Miller formulated his position on the nature and function
of tragedy. The tragic feeling, he writes, is evoked in us when we are
in the presence of a character who is ready to lay down his life, if need
be, to secure one thing—his sense of personal dignity. From Orestes to
Hamlet the underlying struggle is that of the individual attempting to
gain his rightful place in his society. Sometimes he is displaced, sometimes he seeks to attain it for the first time, but the fateful wound
from which all events spiral is the wound of indignity. Man's failure
to achieve or to maintain this needed sense of personal dignity is, according to Miller, the fault of society. He cautions us not to exclude the
personal factor, for the hero must not be flawless, nor ought we to exclude social factors and seek the source of misery solely in our minds.
His emphasis, however, is undoubtedly on the social forces, not on the
hero's inner weakness. Tragedy need not preach revolution, but since
its theme is man's need to wholly realize himself, whatever confines man
and stunts his growth is "ripe for attack and examination." Man's destruction in his effort to evaluate himself and to be evaluated justly, says

Miller, "posits a wrong or an evil in his environment." This truth, he adds, is the morality of a tragedy and its lesson, and the enlightenment of a tragedy consists in this discovery of the moral law, not the discovery of some abstract or metaphysical quality. This emphasis on social forces is seen also in Miller's brief but revealing comment on the nature of the tragic flaw. Since the tragic action stems from the questioning of the stable and stifling environment, the importance of the personal flaw is diminished. Indeed, for Miller, this factor in the hero's composition is not necessarily a weakness. It is, he says, man's inherent unwillingness to remain passive in the face of what he conceives to be a challenge to his dignity, his image of his rightful status. Only the passive or submissive are flawless. Thus the accepted notion of the tragic flaw as a shortcoming in the hero's character which precipitates the catastrophic action and which, theoretically at least, makes morally tolerable his defeat, is transformed by Miller into what would seem to be a condition of the hero's greatness.

Thus, for the most part in this essay, Miller sees the human situation as the product of forces outside the individual person and the tragedy inherent in the situation as a consequence of the individual's total onslaught against an order that degrades. The function of tragedy is to reveal the truth concerning our society, which frustrates and denies man his right to personal dignity; and the enlightenment of tragedy is the discovery of the moral law that supports this right. Basically the aesthetic position formulated in "Tragedy and the Common Man" is influenced, perhaps even determined, by Miller the social critic, and while the terms of this definition of tragedy are acceptable, they are also limited.

Miller's first play, *All My Sons,* reveals this concern with social issues. It is most clearly and simply in the tradition of the social problem plays of Ibsen, Shaw, and Galsworthy. An aspect of the tragedy arises out of the character of the son, Chris Keller, out of an inner conflict between the affection and loyalty he had for his father and his concept of justice and universal brotherhood which the father offended. The persons in the play, however, exist mainly to illustrate the unhappy consequences of a disaster generated by a selfish, materialistic society which respects economic success as it flaunts underlying moral law. At the climax of the play, Joe Keller comes to realize that all the young soldiers killed or endangered by his selfish action are his sons as much as are his own two boys for whom he was building up his business. And in reply to the mother's cry at the end of the play, "What more can we be?", Chris, the remaining son, says, "You can be better! Once, for all, you can know there's a universe of people outside and you're responsible to it, and unless you know that, you threw away your son because that's why he died." The play advances clearly to this punch-line.

In *Death of a Salesman* we find the same emphasis on social forces as the source of tragedy, though the issue here is somewhat confused by Miller's attempt to make of Willy Loman a tragic hero. The essay "Tragedy and the Common Man," published in 1949, the same year that *Death of a Salesman* appeared, has obvious application to the play. Miller in general terms defends the use of the common man as a fit subject for tragedy in the highest sense, as rank is not a measure of human greatness. Insistence upon rank, he says, is but a clinging to outward forms of tragedy. In the conflict the hero gains "size," that tragic stature that is spuriously attached to the high born in our minds. The commonest of men may take on that stature to the extent of his willingness to throw all he has into the contest—the battle to secure his rightful place in his world. The idea that a tragedy can be based on the lives of ordinary folk is not new in the modern period. Ibsen's drama and Synge's *Riders to the Sea* are obvious examples. What is interesting here is that Miller in the essay makes a case for the common man protagonist, the low man, as tragic hero. He is a man who struggles against "a seemingly stable cosmos" to secure what he conceives his rights, to preserve his dignity. This is closer to the traditional view of tragedy, with its focus on the individual. But, while we may be prepared to accept the argument that a common man, that is, one without rank, may achieve heroic stature, the tragic nature of *Death of a Salesman* does not stem from this possibility. Willy Loman does not gain "size" from the situation. He is seen primarily as the victim of his society; his warped values, the illusions concerning the self he projects, reflect those of his society. His moments of clear self-knowledge are few, and even fewer are the moments when he asserts with strength and dignity his worthwhileness—that of the common man—as he does when he angrily rejects Biff's estimate of himself and his father ("Pop, I'm a dime a dozen and so are you") with his cry "I am not a dime a dozen! I am Willy Loman and you are Biff Loman!" Though there are occasions, too, when Willy emerges from the fog of self-deception and illusion, when he sees himself clearly—and at the end he does realize that Biff loves him for himself alone—he goes to his death clinging to his illusions. He is a pathetic figure, yet Miller in his essay written at this time says that there is no place for pathos in real tragedy. Pathos, he remarks, is the mode for the pessimist, suitable for the kind of struggle where man is obviously doomed from the outset. And earlier in the essay Miller postulated that tragedy must be inherently optimistic. In Miller's view of the nature of tragedy and his expression of it in his plays, there seems to be some confusion that needs to be examined.

In *All My Sons* we have a tragedy in the manner of the modern problem play. After this Miller seemed to be moving towards a greater emphasis on character. In "Tragedy and the Common Man" not only does he say that the common man may have heroic stature, but he implies that in tragedy he must have it, and that the tragic effect stems from the hero's struggle against the conventions, persons, and institutions ranged against him. But Miller's concern is still largely with those forces which he wished to condemn and with establishing the underlying moral law or a principle that could serve as an alternative to the prevailing social condition which shapes, or rather maims us. This is made clear in a passage in the Introduction to his *Collected Plays,* where Miller says that the tragedy in *Death of a Salesman* grows out of the fact that

> Willy Loman has broken a law without whose protection life is insupportable if not imcomprehensible to him and to many others; it is a law which says that a failure in society and in business has no right to live. Unlike the law against incest, the law of success is not administered by a statute or church, but it is very nearly as powerful in its grip upon men. The confusion increases because, while it is a law, it is by no means a wholly agreeable one even as it is slavishly obeyed, for to fail is no longer to belong to society, in his estimate. Therefore, the path is open for those who wish to call Willy merely a foolish man even as they themselves are living in obedience to the same law that killed him.

And so in *Death of a Salesman,* though Willy is as prominent as a tragic hero in the action, he never achieves heroic stature because of Miller's too strong concern with criticism of his society. The social problem play that would express this criticism leads him to present Willy as a nearly always deluded victim rather than as a sufficiently clear-sighted heroic challenger.

The same dichotomy persists in *The Crucible* between the concept of tragedy evidenced in the problem play, with the focus of interest on social conditions that are expressed through characters and their interactions, and the pre-modern, or what has been called the Christian tragedy, in which the focus of attention is on the tragic hero and the social context is given what significance it has through its bearing on him. Though *The Crucible* is a very powerful drama, structurally it suffers from Miller's failure to resolve this confusion. The introduction which outlines the social context, the opening scene, and large sections of the play later provide more than a background before which the protagonist acts. They have a significance greater than necessary for the playing out of the tragedy of John Proctor. The diffusion of the tragic force that results from the dramatist presenting the evil in society crushing Giles Corey, Rebecca Nurse, and others, as well as John Proctor, supports this view. Miller is clearly interested in showing the larger social effects of the particular blight that concerns him here. Even though we can agree with him that *The Crucible* is not merely a response to McCarthyism, or an attempt to cure witch-hunting, any more than the intention of *Death of a Salesman* is to improve conditions for travellers, nevertheless the concern with the political problem was obvious when the play appeared in 1953. Indeed Miller, in an article on *The Crucible,* reiterates his earlier statement that the dramatist cannot consider man apart from his social context and the problems that his environment presents. "I believe," he writes, "that it is no longer possible to contain the truth of the human situation so totally within a single man's guts as the bulk of our plays presuppose." It is not merely that man and the environment interact, but that they are part of each other—"The fish is in the water and the water is in the fish." We in the twentieth century, Miller adds, are more aware than any preceding generation "of the larger units that help make us and destroys us. . . . The vast majority of us know now—not merely as knowledge but as feeling, feeling capable of expression in art—that we are being formed, that our alternatives in life are not absolutely our own, as the romantic play inevitably must presuppose." Then, with specific reference to *The Crucible,* he says further, "The form, the shape, the meaning of *The Crucible* were all compounded out of the faith of those who were hanged. They were asked to be lonely and they refused. . . . It was not good to cast this play, to form it so that the psyche of the hero should emerge so 'commonly' as to wipe out of mind the process itself, the spectacle of that faith. . . ."

And yet the play, after the opening scene, becomes increasingly concerned with the role of one man, John Proctor, and the crisis that is inner, though prompted by outside forces. The intensity of the tragedy results from this increasing concentration on the individual, the tragic hero, who, in his dilemma, epitomizes the whole tragic situation. Whether

Miller intended it or not, the play compels us to focus on Proctor (unfortunately not always), and through him we realize most clearly Miller's theme, which, as he also tells us, is "the conflict between a man's raw deeds and his conception of himself; the question of whether conscience is in fact an organic part of the human being, and what happens when it is handed over not merely to the state or the mores of the time but to one's friend or wife. The big difference, I think, is that *The Crucible* sought to include a higher degree of consciousness than the earlier plays." This higher degree of consciousness is very important, as it raises the stature of the hero, makes him a worthier protagonist, and renders more significant the role of will. Only if the hero knows the issue and sees clearly his position can his struggle become a clear expression of will and character. Only when the will is conscious can it be heroic and the protagonist become more than a victim like Willy Loman, whose will to resist degrading conditions is really nullified by his acceptance of them —an acceptance made possible by his very limited vision.

Though *The Crucible* was undoubtedly prompted in part by a contemporary political situation for which the Salem witch-hunt was an apt counterpart, and though Miller may well have intended to write a tragic problem play, he seems to have become increasingly concerned with and even carried away by the tragedy in individual human terms. Indeed in the Introduction to his *Collected Plays* Miller tells us that it was an individual's crisis, not a social issue, that precipitated the play:

> I doubt that I should ever have tempted agony by actually writing a play on the subject (the Salem witch-hunt) had I not come upon a single fact. It was that Abigail Williams, the prime mover of the Salem hysteria, so far as the hysterical children were concerned, had a short time earlier been the house servant of the Proctors and now was crying out Elizabeth Proctor as a witch; but more—it was clear from the record that with entirely uncharacteristic fastidiousness she was refusing to include John Proctor, Elizabeth's husband, in her accusations despite the urgings of the prosecutors.

Miller's increasing concern with the individual rather than with the social issue, or rather his attempt to express the issue primarily through a clearly and intensely conceived character with heroic qualities, while evident in *The Crucible*, is carried even further in *A View from the Bridge*. Here too fate is seen to some extent as external to man, a condition of environment. But here it is expressed largely through individual persons rather than conventions and institutions, through a coming together of persons whose presence takes on dramatic significance only in relation to the protagonist. And Miller has no easy explanation for the fateful interplay. In an article which appeared in the *New York Times* (September 25, 1955), he wrote:

> There was such an iron-bound purity in the autonomic egocentricity of the aims of each of the persons involved that the weaving together of their lives seemed almost the work of a fate. I have tried to press as far as my reason can go toward defining the objective and subjective elements that made that fate, but I must confess that in the end a mystery remains for me.

The illegal immigrants, the two women in the play—Eddie's wife and his niece—important as they are to the plot, even the moral law by which Eddie lives and of which he runs afoul, all take their importance from the way in which they precipitate Eddie's passion and are the agency of his destruction. Eddie's attractiveness or unattractiveness, his rightness or his essential wrongness become relatively unimportant. What counts is that here is a man who, as Miller says, "possesses or exemplifies the wondrous or humane fact that he too can be driven to what in the last analysis is a sacrifice of himself for his conception, however misguided, of right, dignity, and justice." Unlike the ending of *All My Sons* with its moral tag that we are all one family and that a selfishness which is prepared to destroy others leads to self-destruction, and unlike the ending of *Death of a Salesman* with Charley's concluding remarks blaming society ("Nobody dast blame this man. A salesman is got to dream, boy"), the conclusion of *A View from the Bridge,* spoken by Alfieri, who serves as a Chorus in the play, emphasizes the tragedy potential in man himself:

> Most of the time now we settle for half and I like it better. But the truth is holy, and even as I know how wrong he was, and his death useless, I tremble, for I confess that something perversely pure calls to me from his memory—not purely good, but himself purely, for he allowed himself to be wholly known and for that I think I will love him more than all my sensible clients. And yet, it is better to settle for half, it must be! And so I mourn him—I admit it—with a certain alarm.

It is interesting to note that in his early essay, "Tragedy and the Common Man," in which Miller stresses the external factors as the source of tragedy, he mentions only the emotion of terror as provoked by the spectacle of the "total onslaught by an individual against a seemingly stable cosmos." He makes no mention of pity. Here, however, in the last play, where his emphasis has shifted and tragedy is seen not as in the problem play as a product of a social condition that can be altered by resolute action but rather as a condition of a great man's nature, the feeling of pity is powerful.

In an essay that appeared in 1945, W. H. Auden remarked that at the end of a Greek play we say "What a pity it had to be this way," while at the end of a Christian tragedy we say "What a pity it had to be this way when it might have been otherwise." In this pithy but somewhat oversimplified generalization Auden points to a significant distinction between the tragedies of the two cultures. In Greek drama the sense of fate, residing for the most part in forces outside of man, is overwhelming. The destiny of the hero is foretold by oracles, or, as we are often reminded, made the consequence of actions by the gods—of their quarrels and judgments. Their action, moreover, is prompted often by events for which the hero is not responsible. In Christian tragedy there is a sense of greater personal freedom implied—man is free, according to a basic assumption commonly accepted, to act morally. The battleground, in the main, is in the hero's soul. In Greek drama the situation is given, fixed, and the dramatist concentrates on the way in which his characters respond to the grip events have on them. In Christian tragedy the situation is not given, or its givenness is irrelevant; the situation is created and destiny is not known beforehand. But there is a fixed system of moral imperatives resting on divine authority, there is an established order, and the tragedy works itself out largely in terms of the hero's conscious or accidental violation of that order. Arthur Miller in his plays combines elements of both. As in Christian drama the situation is not given; but as in Greek drama, the forces making for tragedy are often outside the protagonist—he is caught in circumstances not of his own making. But unlike Greek drama, these forces that determine or are the fate of the protagonist are not beyond his reach. Hence the possibility of decisive action is held out, and the will of the hero is called into play. Furthermore, Miller becomes decreasingly concerned with external factors until in *A View from the Bridge* the focus of attention is almost entirely on the central character, Eddie Carbone, and the way in which he confronts his situation. Yet in other respects *A View from the Bridge* is the most classical of Miller's tragedies. The use of the engaged narrator, or Chorus, to underline the generalized significance of the play and the depiction of the hero as a man almost possessed, driven beyond the ultimate bound of caution to destruction by an overwhelming force, strongly reminds us of Greek tragedy. But we do not feel that he is destined to defeat. As

in Christian drama, we feel that the possibility for self-mastery is there—
that is, it might have been otherwise.

Miller's tragedies then tend to fluctuate, often uneasily, between Greek
drama with its emphasis on external causes (though Miller tries to avoid
its fatalism) and Christian drama, which involves freedom and responsibility and which seeks the source of tragedy in the individual. His drama
is unlike both in that for the most part it rejects a religious framework.
Miller, like most modern tragedians, has been seeking a new explanation
of the human situation with its tragic aspects. He seeks it in naturalistic
and humanistic terms, not transcendental ones. Our ignorance, our lack
of consciousness, is remediable. Our man-made ethical system, though
incomplete and faulty, can be improved. Our environment, which re-
stricts and defeats us, which prevents us from realizing ourselves (a failure
which to Miller is the heart of the tragic experience) can be changed—
if we will. The modern dramatists have to postulate a free will in what
appears as an otherwise mechanistic world. This is one of the dilemmas
faced by the writers of problem plays. Insofar as they regard external
factors as the source of tragedy and regard man as largely the product
and victim of his environment, they would seem to negate the idea of
an effective free will. But this they are disinclined to do. For the most
part the determinism that is implied in the naturalist view of man is
ignored, and instead the view is presented that man is not merely a part
of nature, but apart from it; that he is not simply subject to its laws and
forces, but can and should resist his environment or fate and seek to
change it. The underlying position is optimistic: that man, an object of
nature, is more than nature; that Willy Loman, for example, can somehow be more than the force that made him. The dilemma, which is
clearly seen in *Death of a Salesman,* was recognized by Arthur Miller in
the concluding paragraphs of his recent and fullest statement, the Introduction to his *Collected Plays*:

> A drama worthy of its time must first, knowingly or by instinctive means,
> recognize its major and most valuable traditions and where it has departed
> from them. Determinism, whether it is based on the iron necessities of eco-
> nomics or on psychoanalytic theory seen as a closed circle, is a contradiction
> of the idea of drama itself as drama has come down to us in its fullest de-
> velopments. The idea of the hero, let alone the mere protagonist, is incom-
> patible with a drama whose bounds are set in advance by the concept of an
> unbreakable trap. Nor is it merely that one wants arbitrarily to find a hero
> and a victory. The history of man is a ceaseless process of overthrowing one

determinism to make way for another more faithful to life's changing relationships. And it is a process inconceivable without the existence of the will of man. His will is as much a fact as his defeat. . . .

The idea of realism has become wedded to the idea that man is at best the sum of forces working upon him and of given psychological forces within him. Yet an innate value, an innate will, does in fact posit itself as real not alone because it is devoutly to be wished, but because, however closely he is measured and systematically accounted for, he is more than the sum of his stimuli and is unpredictable beyond a certain point. A drama, like a history, which stops at this point, the point of conditioning, is not reflecting reality. What is wanted, therefore, is not a poetry of escape from process and determinism, like that mood play which stops where feeling ends or that inverted romanticism which would mirror all the world in the sado-masochistic relationship. Nor will the heightening of the intensity of language alone yield the prize. A new poem will appear because a new balance has been struck which embraces both determinism and the paradox of will. If there is one unseen goal toward which every play in this book strives, it is that very discovery and its proof—that we are made and yet more than what made us.

On this note of faith, which well reflects the direction in which Arthur Miller has been moving, it might be well to end. In most respects Miller's position now is what it was ten years ago. He has been consistent in rejecting an exclusive preoccupation with the individual in terms of his neuroses or other purely private concerns, or with an exclusive preoccupation with social forces. He was always conscious not merely of their interplay, but of their fusion. But there has been an appreciable alteration in his angle of vision that has resulted in a sharper focussing on the individual and the subordination of the social issue to the inner crisis. As he moves towards greater emphasis on character, Miller has been making the protagonist a worthier opposite to the forces he struggles against. He has been giving his common man tragic stature, and the result has been a strengthening and an intensifying of the tragic quality in his plays.

Point of View in Arthur Miller's
Death of a Salesman

by Brian Parker

I

In *Death of a Salesman* Arthur Miller wrote far better than he seems to have realized, at least, if we may judge by his critical essays on the play.[1] This is true of both the play's content—its analysis of American values—and of its technique. Miller's recent *After the Fall* uses the same non-logical, subjective memory structure as the earlier play, and uses it far more consistently and skillfully, and yet is far less effective in engaging the self-identification by the audience for which expressionism strives. And this is not only because the experience examined in *After the Fall* is less common than the disaster of Willy Loman, but because the very hesitancies of technique in *Death of a Salesman,* its apparent uncertainty in apportioning realism and expressionism, provide a dramatic excitement of a more complex kind than Miller achieves in his later, more consistent plays.

To claim to understand a play better than its author does may sound egotistic, but we may take comfort from the fact that Miller himself says *j* in the Preface to his *Collected Plays*:

> . . . a writer of any worth creates out of his total perception, the vaster proportion of which is subjective and not within his intellectual control

"Point of View in Arthur Miller's *Death of a Salesman*" by Brian Parker. From *University of Toronto Quarterly*, XXXV (January, 1966), 144–57. Reprinted by permission of Brian Parker and the *University of Toronto Quarterly*.

[1]Preface, *Arthur Miller's Collected Plays* (New York, 1960); *Death of a Salesman*: a symposium," *Tulane Drama Review*, II (1958); "Tragedy and the Common Man," *Theatre Arts*, XXXV (1951), 48–50.

. . . if it is art [that the playwright] has created, it must by definition bend itself to his observation rather than to his opinions *or even his hopes.*[2]

It is the contention of this paper, therefore, that by keeping close to actual observation *Death of a Salesman* presents a far more accurate weighing of American values than Miller's subsequent analyses suggest and that the blurred line between realism and expressionism is not the weakness some critics have claimed, but, on the contrary, one of the play's most subtle successes.

II

The realism in *Death of a Salesman* is fairly obvious, and reflects the influence on Miller of Henrik Ibsen, the Ibsen, that is, of the middle phase, the great realist reformer. In *All My Sons* and *Death of a Salesman* Miller adopts Ibsen's "retrospective" structure, in which an explosive situation in the present is both explained and brought to a crisis by the gradual revelation of something which has happened in the past: in *Death of a Salesman* this is, of course, Willy Loman's adultery, which by alienating his son, Biff, has destroyed the strongest value in Willy's life. This structure is filled out with a detailed evocation of modern, urban, lower-middle-class life: Miller documents a world of arch-supports, aspirin, spectacles, subways, time payments, advertising, Chevrolets, faulty refrigerators, life insurance, mortgages, and the adulation of high school football heroes. The language, too, except in a few places which will be considered later, is an accurate record of the groping, half inarticulate, cliché-ridden inadequacy of ordinary American speech. And the deadly realism of the picture is confirmed for us by the way that American audiences have immediately recognized and identified with it in the theatre.

However, even in his realist plays, Ibsen has details which, while still being acceptably probable, have also a deeper, symbolic significance: one thinks of such things as the polluted swimming baths in *An Enemy of the People,* the eponymous wild duck, or, more abstractly, the hair and

[2] Preface, *Arthur Miller's Collected Plays,* 36–37; see also 8: ". . . in his conscious intention the artist often conceals from himself an aim which can be quite opposed to his fondest beliefs and desires."

pistols motifs in *Hedda Gabler*. Such a deepening of realism is also a
technique in *Death of a Salesman*. Consider, for instance, the value that
Willy and his sons attach to manual work, and its glamorous extension,
sport, their belief that it is necessary for a man to keep fit, to be able to
handle tools and build things. Willy's handiness around the house is
constantly impressed on us: "He was always good with his hands,"
Linda remembers, and Biff says that his father put more enthusiasm into
building the stoop than into all his salesmanship; in his reveries Willy
again teaches his boys how to simonize a car the most efficient way, and
is contemptuous of his neighbour Charlie, and Charlie's son Bernard,
because they lack the manual skills; Willy's favourite son, Biff, is even
more dextrous than his father—in high school he was a star athlete and,
as a man, he can find happiness only as a ranch hand; one remembers
that Willy's father was a pioneer type who drove over the country in a
wagon, earning money by ingenious inventions and the making of flutes.
Willy's mystique of physical skill is thus a reflection of the simpler,
pioneer life he craves, a symptom and a symbol of his revolt against the
constraints of the modern city.

Slightly more abstract, yet still realistic, is the play's use of trees to
symbolize the rural way of life which modern commercialism is choking.
Willy, we are told, bought his house originally because it stood in a
wooded suburb where he could hunt a little, and where his yard was
flanked by two great elms; but now the trees have been cut down and his
property is so over-shadowed by apartment houses that he cannot even
grow seed in his back garden. (The choked seed is a fairly obvious
symbol: Willy Loman is trapped in a society which prevents him establishing anything to outlast himself, ruining the lives of his sons as well
as his own.) We learn at the beginning that it is dreaming about the
countryside and watching scenery, particularly trees, which is the main
cause of Willy's recent road accidents; it is to look after timber that
Willy's brother, Ben, tries to persuade him to go to Alaska; the "jungle,"
Ben says, is the place for riches; and at moments of crisis Willy yells
"The woods are burning," a phrase which is nonsensical unless seen in
context of the other tree references.

The last example is already diverging from realism: that is, it is not
a phrase habitually used in American life; it needs the context of the
play to give it meaning. And when we find Miller directing that, whenever Willy remembers the past, the stage be drenched in a green, check-

ered pattern of leaves, then it is obvious that the technique has moved
from realistic symbolism to outright expressionism.[3]

The set for the play, designed by Jo Mielziner but to Miller's specifi-
cations, and influenced, no doubt, by the set for O'Neill's *Desire under
the Elms,* is a bizarre but wholly successful mingling of realism and
non-realism. Its skeletal house shows several rooms simultaneously (like
mediaeval staging); the house is sparsely furnished with just enough properties to suggest a sense of place and environment,[4] with the result, as
the first stage direction suggests, that "an air of dream clings to the
place, a dream rising out of reality"; and the house has in front of it a
bare, neutral forestage, used (as in the Elizabethan theatre) to represent
any place demanded by the story, with necessary props being carried on
and off by the characters themselves. The skeletal framework of the
house also gives it a sense of fragility which is intensified by surrounding
it with the menacing silhouettes of tall apartment houses, producing an
effect of claustrophobia, of rural wood menaced by asphalt jungle.

The set is expressionistically lit to reinforce this impression. The
apartment silhouettes are bathed in angry orange; when Willy remembers the past, the house is dappled by the green of vanished trees; when
Biff and Hap pick up two women and neglect their father, the directions request a lurid red; and at the end, when Willy insanely tries to
plant seed by night, the "blues" of the stage direction simultaneously
suggests moonlight and his mood of despair. Music is similarly manipulated: the rural way of life is represented by flute music, telling "of grass
and trees and the horizon"; it is heard only by Willy whenever he dreams
of the life he should have led or of the early days when his suburb was
still in the country. It is associated, of course, with Willy's pioneer father,
the flute maker; and in the modern world has degenerated to Willy and
Biff's unbusinesslike habit of whistling in elevators, and, at a yet further
remove, to the mechanized whistling of Howard and his children as
played back on a tape recorder. The tape recorder scene is, in fact, a
brilliantly compact piece of symbolism, functioning like the "mirror
scene" in some of Shakespeare's plays (or Brecht's *"Grundgestus"*) to

[3] The 1963 production at the Tyrone Guthrie Theatre in Minneapolis suffered because it emphasized the realistic aspects of the play and cut down the expressionistic.
There were no apartment silhouettes, for example, nor any manipulation of lighting
or music.

[4] All the properties listed in the original stage direction are used or referred to in the
course of the play, except the athletic trophy whose symbolic purpose is obvious anyway.

epitomize the action of the whole play: not only does it illustrate the mechanization of family life, but Howard's idolizing of his children and bullying of his wife exactly parallel Willy's, showing a resemblance between the two men which undercuts left-wing clichés about employer and worker; and, when Willy knocks it over and cannot stop it, the machine serves as both cause and illustration of Willy's mental break-down: he has one of his schizophrenic attacks, and the mechanical voices, so like those of his own home life, are an equivalent to the clamorous subconscious of which he has also lost control. The crucial hotel bedroom scene, in which Biff discovers his father's adultery, is heralded by a shrill trumpet blast, and Willy's final disaster is conveyed by musical shorthand: his decision to commit suicide is accompanied by a prolonged, maddening note, which collapses into a crash of discords, to represent the car crash offstage, and then modulates into a dead march to introduce the requiem scene. Certain characters and situations also have what amount to *leit-motifs:* besides the flute music, we are told there is a "boys' music"; raucous sex music for the scene of Biff's dis-covery and the barroom scene where Biff and Hap pick up women; and a special music to herald the appearances in Willy's memory of his elder brother, Ben.

The presentation of Ben is an important clue as to exactly how, and why, Miller is using expressionism in *Death of a Salesman*. He is dis-tinctly less "real" than the other characters of the play, stiffer, with a more stilted way of speaking: in the original production, Elia Kazan had the part acted unnaturally, like an automaton. Ben seems less "real" than the others because he is not so much a person as the embodiment of Willy's desire for escape and success: Willy calls him "success in-carnate." This is proved by the fact that he does not only appear in memory scenes but is summoned up at the end to "discuss" Willy's plan of suicide; obviously, he here represents a side of Willy's own mind. It is interesting to note, therefore, that the stage directions emphasize that Ben always appears at exactly the moment Willy thinks of him, which is not true of the other characters in the memory scenes. The figure of Ben, then, represents not Ben as he actually was, so much as Ben as his image has been warped in the mind of the rememberer, Willy; and this reveals the peculiar nature of expressionism in *Death of a Salesman*.

Miller is not using expressionistic techniques in the way they are used by the German writers of the 1920's, to dramatize abstract forces in politics or economics or history. He is using the techniques solely as a means of revealing the character of Willy Loman,[5] the values Willy holds and, particularly, the way his mind works. Miller's reason for blending realism and expressionism in *Death of a Salesman* is that this combination reflects the protagonist's actual way of thinking: "I wished to create a form," says Miller, "which . . . would literally be the process of Willy Loman's mind." [6] It is Willy Loman's character, therefore, which is the chief link between the two dramatic modes, and this is possible, of course, because Willy is technically a schizophrenic: overwork, worry and, particularly, repressed guilt have resulted in a mental breakdown in which present and past mingle for him inextricably, where, in Miller's own phrase, time is "exploded."

As Miller points out,[7] this is not a "flashback" technique (the film of *Death of a Salesman* failed precisely because it tried to turn the memory sequences into flashbacks); what it does is to present a past distorted by the rememberer's mind—a subjective, not objective record; and the memories have an extra tension because they occur simultaneously with events in the present, more like a double exposure than a flashback. Note, for instance, how the memory scenes appear gradually, usurping the present bit by bit in the card game with Charlie when Willy is talking to the remembered Ben and the actual Charlie simultaneously, or the gradual emergence of the repressed hotel bedroom scene which is brought to a climax when Biff's and Happy's pick-ups enter in the present. This simultaneous presentation of past and present, dream and reality, gives the play a metaphoric quality, a Cocteau-ish "poetry of the theatre," which (in my opinion) compensates for the so often criticized banality of language. Ambiguity, irony, and tension occur in the action and stage pictures, not in the wording where they might, more conventionally, be expected. It is a metaphor in time.

The form of the play, then, depends on the gradual admission by Willy *to himself* of his own guilt; it differs from the public exposés of Ibsen's form in that Willy's adultery is never openly discussed between him and Biff, and Linda and Hap never learn of it at all: the sole importance is that Willy himself should recognize it. Normal chronology is ignored, therefore: the order of events depends on the way that memories of the past swim up out of Willy's memory because of their emotional association with things happening in the present. For example,

---

[5] See Preface, *Collected Plays*, 39.
[6] *Ibid.*, 23–24.
[7] *Ibid.*, 26.

Willy's worry about having nearly crashed his car in the present brings up memories of happy experiences with cars in the past; as Willy eases his feeling of inferiority to Charlie by mocking Charlie's lack of skill with tools, this conjures up the memory of Ben, Willy's ideal of practical success, and leads with emotional but not chronological logic to reminiscences of their pioneer father. Note, particularly, that certain things always "trigger" this kind of mental relapse in Willy because they are associated with his guilt: silk stockings, for instance, or the sound of women laughing; and the blurring of mental realities is represented usually by characters stepping across the wall lines of the skeletal setting. Miller says: ". . . the structure of the play was determined by what was needed to draw up [Willy's] memories like a mass of tangled roots without end or beginning." This provides a sense of climax because "if I could make him remember enough he would kill himself." [8]

However, Miller's explanation of his purpose fails to account for an important inconsistency in the use of expressionism. The play does not divide neatly into realistic scenes in the present and expressionistic memory scenes in Willy's mind; some of the expressionistic scenes deal with events in the present when Willy is not even there, and cannot therefore be said to be distorted through his schizophrenia. Consider the scenes downtown in Howard's office or the barroom, before Willy arrives, which are represented nonrealistically on the unlocalized forestage; or, most strikingly, the unrealism of the "Requiem" scene, where characters break the wall lines to come downstage, and the forestage itself represents a graveyard. This cannot be a distortion of Willy's mind because Willy is already dead.

The rationale behind the mingling of realism and expressionism is thus uncertain. The result is intriguing. The extension of expressionism to non-memory scenes means that we see even events which Willy did not experience as though through Willy's eyes, as Willy *might* have experienced them. The play's technique thus forces the audience to become Willy Lomans for the whole duration of the play, to sympathize with his predicament in a way they could not do in real life. It allows them to see more than Willy does, but not to see more than he might have seen; they are expected to criticize Willy, but the technique forces them to criticize him from within, as Willy criticizes and condemns himself. Miller tells us some interesting facts about the genesis of the play which are relevant here:

[8] *Ibid.*, 25.

The first image that occurred to me which was to result in *Death of a Sales-man* was an enormous face to the height of the proscenium arch which would appear and then open up, and we would see the inside of a man's head. In fact, *The Inside of His Head* was the first title. It was conceived half in laughter, for the inside of his head was a mass of contradictions.[9]

The last sentence is particularly important because it reflects on the values of the play in a way which has not yet been analysed: if we see *all* the play as Willy might have experienced it, even those scenes in which he does not actually appear, then *all* the values of the play, good as well as bad, will be restricted to values which Willy might himself have held. The frame of values will be relative to the potential of a character like Willy's, adjusted to the limits of his imagination. This important "point of view" in the play has been invariably neglected; discussions of *Death of a Salesman* assume that it presents Miller's own values, and Miller's defence of Willy as a tragic hero has done nothing to rectify the error.

III

Obviously, *Death of a Salesman* is a criticism of the moral and social standards of contemporary America, not merely a record of the particular plight of one man. And, also obviously, it presents Willy as a victim of the deterioration of the "American dream," the belief in untrammelled individualism. The word "dream" is a key word, recurring frequently in the play; and the deterioration of American individualism is traced through the Loman generations in a descending scale, from the Whit-man-like exuberance of Willy's father, through Ben, Willy himself, to the empty predatoriness of Happy, who is, he admits, compulsively com-petitive in sex and business for no reason at all.

The ideal of self-dependence has become the vicious competition of the modern business community, of which Willy, as a salesman, is the lowest common denominator. Miller has explained Willy's surname as standing for "low man on the totem pole," the bottom of the heap; and interestingly, Willy's ideal, the old salesman in green slippers, is called "Dave *Single*man." The two names contrast Willy's actual exploitation and the dignified independence to which he aspired.

[9] *Ibid.*, 23.

Willy's philosophy is the personality cult of Dale Carnegie, the "win friends and influence people" theory which exploits human relations for purposes of gain. "Be liked and you will never want," Willy advises his sons; and his famous distinction between being "liked" and being "well liked" seems to rest on whether or not the liking can be exploited for practical ends. Such using of friendliness falsifies it and invokes a law of diminishing returns, as Willy's lonely funeral shows. The attitude also encourages empty dreams, reflected economically in advertising and time-payments; it is essentially parasitic, producing, building, planting nothing; and the logical extension of its unrestrained competition is Biff's downright theft. The psychologists explain theft as a form of love substitute; and it is true that Biff's stealing only becomes obsessive after his disillusion with Willy; but much more important is the fact that in the past Willy not only condoned but tacitly encouraged Biff's stealing of a football and lumber from a building lot. Willy's bluffing advice to Biff: "Remember, start big and you'll end big," is startlingly like the dictum of the late notorious Dr. Stephen Ward: "If you want to succeed, start at the top!"

So far, then, the play presents a rather conventional, if very powerful, expression of left-wing attitudes to capitalism which have been common since the 1930's.[10] However, *Death of a Salesman* cannot be simplified into mere propaganda. The naïve interpretation of Willy Loman's plight as the result of exploitation of workers by capitalists is qualified in the play in several important ways. In the first place, Willy's employer, Howard, is not presented as a conscious monster but as a man very like Willy himself, with the same narrow love for his family, the same love of gadgetry, the same empty friendliness. Handy-dandy, which is the master, which is the man? The resemblance of the two men suggests that the basic error must be sought in human nature, not just in a particular economic system. Secondly, Willy's plight is shown to be at least partly the result of his own character; he fails not only because of the pressure of the competitive system, but also because of his incorrigible inability to tell the truth even to himself, his emotional, nonlogical mode of thought, which allows him flatly to contradict himself, and of which schizophrenia is merely an intensification: where once he confused reality and wish fulfillment, he now confuses reality and an

[10] Clifford Odets' *Awake and Sing!* has a somewhat similar situation to *Death of a Salesman*: a grandfather commits suicide so his grandson may use the insurance money to fulfill the immigrant dreams the grandfather himself failed to achieve.

idealized past] Thirdly, the play balances the failure of Willy and his
children with the success of Charlie and his son, Bernard, who thrive
in the very same system: Charlie and his son do not cheat, they merely
work hard; they prosper yet remain kindly, unpretentious, sensitive,
helpful. Their presence in the play destroys any interpretation of *Death
of a Salesman* as left-wing propaganda. In fact, the exaggerated nature
of Bernard's success suggests that Miller partially shares the "American
dream" himself; and he has been accused of making a merely vulgar
distinction between successful materialism in Charlie and Bernard and
unsuccessful in Willy.

However, no consideration of the positive values in *Death of a Salesman* is fair unless it takes into account the play's peculiar point of view.
This is the area where the distinction between Miller's observation and
the limitations of the Loman sensibility through which the whole play
is strained becomes most delicate to trace. The positive values suggested
in the play are only such as Willy himself might have arrived at; and
it is my purpose to suggest that, deliberately or not, Miller presents them
as necessarily limited ideals.

IV

The futile philosophy of Willy Loman is opposed by three main alternatives in *Death of a Salesman*: the pioneering adventurousness of Ben,
the sensible practicality of Charlie, and the loyalty of Linda—to list them
in order of progressive importance. The values represented by Ben need
not detain us very long. Their inadequacy is apparent. Miller's work,
as a whole, does reflect a certain admiration for the pioneer virtues of
courage and self-reliance, but this is matched by an awareness that such
attitudes are dangerous in modern society: the aggressiveness which is
admirable in combatting raw nature becomes immoral when turned
against one's fellow men. It is the latter, critical attitude which predominates in Miller's picture of Ben, who advises Biff: "Never fight fair
with a stranger, boy. You'll never get out of the jungle that way." Clearly,
if Willy had gone with Ben to Alaska, he might have been a richer, but
he would not have been a better man.

The values represented by Charlie are more important. Charlie is
presented as an almost completely sympathetic figure, but Miller includes
a few details which prevent any acceptance of Charlie's career as ideal.

In the first place, it is suggested, by Charlie himself, that he has had
to pay a certain price for his business success, the price of not caring:
"My salvation is that I never took an interest in anything." In human
terms, Willy's ideal of business, represented by old Dave Singleman,
though it is disastrously inaccurate, is more generous than Charlie's
calm assurance that "The only thing you got in this world is what you
can sell"; it is not without significance that, whereas Willy's idols are
the millionaire inventors Edison and Gooderich (one remembers that
Willy's father was an inventor), Charlie's is the buccaneer financier,
J. P. Morgan. This difference in human warmth between Willy and
Charlie comes out in Charlie's tight-lipped reticence, remarked on by
Willy as a contrast to his own inability to refrain from chatter. However,
the conclusive rebuttal of Charlie's acceptance of the business world
comes in the "Requiem": his defence of Willy in the "Nobody dast
blame this man" speech, which romanticizes the salesman whose job
requires him to dream great things, is immediately rejected by Biff, who
maintains that Willy was to blame because he lacked self knowledge,
because his dreams were all the wrong dreams, because he let himself
be caught in an inhuman system. For all his sympathetic qualities,
therefore, Charlie's position is shown to be a compromise: he has succeeded by fitting his character into the existing system, meeting business
on its own cold terms. But Biff argues that such a system is too small
for a man as imaginative and emotional as Willy. The implication of
the "Requiem" is not that Willy ought to have behaved like Charlie,
but that he should not have been in business at all.

The most powerful positive value in the play is the value of family
loyalty. There is no doubt of Willy's love for his family, particularly
for his son, Biff. It is the betrayal of this loyalty which ruins Willy's
life, rather than commercial failure, and it is in the name of family love
that he finally kills himself, dying "as a father, not as a salesman." [11] But,
perhaps because he romanticizes his own father, whom he never knew,
Willy has a false ideal of fatherhood, exposed most blatantly at the very
moment when he decides to sacrifice himself for Biff: "Ben, he'll worship
me for it." Parental love which is really a disguised form of egotism is
a recurrent theme in Miller's work, and the explanation he finds for it is
revealed in Willy's reply when Charlie tells him to forget about Biff:
"Then what have I got to remember?" As the captain in Strindberg's

[11] John Gassner, introduction to *Death of a Salesman* in *Treasury of the Theatre*
(New York, 1961), II, 1061.

The Father says, children are a materialist's only hope of immortality. But this puts an unfair pressure on the children which perverts a true family relationship.

It is not just Willy's egotism which qualifies the family love in *Death of a Salesman*, however; it is also the fact that it is used as an excuse to ignore other, wider loyalties. And this surely is the great limitation of Linda.

Linda is the most sympathetic character in the play. Her famous "attention, attention must be paid" speech is terribly moving in the theatre, perhaps too moving: Miller has said that his great temptation as an artist is that he finds it too easy to write pathos. And Linda is so sympathetic not only because she is the loyal, downtrodden wife, but also because her attitude seems to sum up many traditional American values. In this connection, I believe no one has yet remarked on the resemblances between *Death of a Salesman* and Robert Frost's poem *The Death of the Hired Man*.[12] Quite apart from the echo in their titles, the situations of the two pieces are strikingly similar: in the Frost poem, the hired man, old Silas, has come "home" ("Something you somehow don't have to deserve") to die: like Willy he is worn out:

> And nothing to look backward to with pride
> And nothing to look forward to with hope.

His employer, Warren, seems at first like Howard in the play, unwilling to keep Silas on because he is too old and unreliable; but Warren's wife, Mary, urges pity in lines which are close to Linda's in both their sentiments and their cadence:

> He never did a thing so very bad
> He don't know why he isn't quite as good
> As anyone. He won't be made ashamed
> To please his brother, worthless though he is.

and she says they must befriend him as they once looked after

> . . . the hound that came a stranger to us
> Out of the woods, worn out upon the trail,

recalling Linda's plea that Willy not be allowed to die like an old dog. Mary is also like Linda in her insistence on maintaining the old man's

---

[12] This resemblance was first pointed out to me by my friend and colleague F. T. Flahiff. Mr. Flahiff, however, does not value the play as highly as I do. Frost's poem was published in 1914 in *North of Boston*.

self-respect; Silas' promises to ditch the meadow and clear the top pasture for Warren are like Willy's boasts of future prosperity, face-savers which neither he nor the others really believe; and Willy's inability to accept help from Charlie as a matter of pride is paralleled by Silas' refusal to appeal to his rich brother who is a neighbouring bank director. Like Willy, old Silas is so exhausted that he rambles in his mind, mixing past and present like a dream: "those days trouble Silas like a dream." In particular, Silas harks back to arguments he had with a young college boy who helped with the haying four years before. They argued about how necessary education is to a man, and Silas feels he got the worst of the argument; he wishes he could at least have taught the boy the practical skill of building a load of hay. The feeling here is a mixture of Willy's attitude to Biff and his reluctant admiration for Bernard. There are several other details where the poem has similar sentiments to the play but in slightly different arrangements: the openings are very similar, in each case an unexpected return, a request for kindness by the loving woman, and the man's affection overlaid by indignation at having been abandoned in the first place, irritably denying his real feeling of responsibility; there is the same Christian-name intimacy, firmly establishing the domestic scale of both play and poem—though the nicknames and diminutives of the play serve the further purpose of conveying the immaturity of Willy's world, on a par with his use of schoolboy slang and the characters telling each other to "grow up"; finally, the most tenuous resemblance is the way that the values represented by the women are associated in both play and poem with the values of unspoiled nature, though this is overt in the poem, implicit in the play. The similarity of the two works, particularly their titles, suggests that Miller was directly influenced by Frost; but even if this is not so, the analogy is still useful in that it highlights the traditional, rural, humane values which Frost hymned his whole career and which the society of *Death of a Salesman* denies. The "hired man" is cared for and pitied; the "salesman" is pitilessly discarded.

Her appeal to these traditional values and her downtrodden, loving loyalty are, however, apt to blind audiences to the essential stupidity of Linda's behaviour. Surely it is both stupid and immoral to encourage the man you love in self-deceit and lies. We are told in the stage directions that Linda has the same values as Willy but that she lacks his energy in pursuing them: it was she who persuaded him not to risk Alaska. Linda does not really believe his dreams—at least not at the point

where we meet her, whatever she may have done earlier; but, without
any higher ideals than Willy, she humours him to keep things going.
The easygoing negativeness of Hap is the same moral sloppiness pushed
one degree farther (Biff is his father's son, Hap is his mother's). After
thirty-five years of marriage, Linda is apparently completely unable to
comprehend her husband: her speech at the graveside (I don't understand; the house is paid for) is not only pathetic, it is also an explanation
of the loneliness of Willy Loman which threw him into other women's
arms.

Interestingly, the basic falsity in Linda reveals itself in the rhetoric
of her "attention, attention must be paid" speech, with its epizeuxis,
inversions, and unnatural cadences. And there is a similar falsity of
tone in the other much criticized speech of the play, Charlie's "Nobody
dast blame this man. . . ." Whether Miller intended it or not, the falsity
of both Linda's loyalty and Charlie's acceptance of business is revealed
in the strained language of their rhapsodies. And a more extreme example of the same false rhetoric, very suggestive when we remember
that Ben is always distorted to suit Willy's mind, is the notorious: "When
I was seventeen I walked into the jungle, and when I was twenty-one
I walked out. And by God I was rich." The falsity of these passages
standing out awkwardly from the drabness of speech elsewhere in the
play, is, I would suggest, totally appropriate. The values represented
by Ben, Charlie, and Linda, though they are more positive than Willy's
Dale Carnegie-ism, are in no sense ideal. They are merely values which
Willy could have imagined,[13] in rhetoric Willy would applaud (as I
have heard Linda's speech applauded in the theatre).

V

Death of a Salesman, in fact, offers almost no sure values. Arthur Miller
appears to recognize this when he says it is a contribution to the "steady
year-by-year documentation of the frustration of man," and he moves
to a more positive position in his next play, *The Crucible.* But even
in *Death of a Salesman* there is one positive gain: Biff at least comes
out of the experience with enhanced self-knowledge: "I know who I

[13] Perhaps this is what Miller is driving at when he says Linda is "made by [Willy]
though he did not know it or believe in it or receive it into himself." Preface, *Collected
Plays,* 30.

am, kid." It is not a proud knowledge, rather an admission of limitation and weakness: Biff admits he will never be a big success in the eyes of the world. But such an admission is the beginning of truth; in religious terms it would be called humility (the Preface to *Collected Plays* and *After the Fall* confirm that Miller's interests are finally religious). Moreover, this humility gained by Biff is related to the sacrifice made by Willy. It has been objected, and admitted by Miller, that Willy's stature as a tragic hero is questionable because he dies still self-deceived. But the new truth is there in Biff, and the extension of expressionistic technique beyond Willy's death unbroken into the "Requiem" binds together the two experiences. The extension of the point of view into scenes where Willy does not appear enables the audience at the end to associate Biff's acceptance with Willy's disaster as a single, coherent, and, I would argue, tragic experience; though the technique is closer to *Everyman* than to *Œdipus Rex*,[14] and the audience's identification with the hero's fate is secured by empathy—emotional manipulation of stage techniques —rather than the more usual method of moral sympathy and admiration.

[14] The play's technique of presenting all events and characters as though strained through Willy's mind resembles the Morality technique in which characters and events are all allegories of the central character's psychomachia.

Linda does nothing to help improve Willy's state, for — ① rarely would she encourage the man she loves in self deceit and lies.

The Liberal Conscience
in *The Crucible*

by *Robert Warshow*

One of the things that have been said of *The Crucible,* Arthur Miller's new play about the Salem witchcraft trials, is that we must not be misled by its obvious contemporary relevance: it is a drama of universal significance. This statement, which has usually a somewhat apologetic tone, seems to be made most often by those who do not fail to place great stress on the play's "timeliness." I believe it means something very different from what it appears to say, almost the contrary, in fact, and yet not quite the contrary either. It means: do not be misled by the play's historical theme into forgetting the main point, which is that "witch trials" are always with us, and especially today; but on the other hand do not hold Mr. Miller responsible either for the inadequacies of his presentation of the Salem trials or for the many undeniable and important differences between those trials and the "witch trials" that are going on now. It is quite true, nevertheless, that the play is, at least in one sense, of "universal significance." Only we must ask what this phrase has come to mean, and whether the quality it denotes is a virtue.

The Puritan tradition, the greatest and most persistent formulator of American simplifications, has itself always contained elements disturbingly resistant to ideological—or even simply rational—understanding. The great debate in American Calvinism over "good works" versus the total arbitrariness of the divine will was won, fortunately and no doubt inevitably, by those who held that an actively virtuous life must be at least the outward sign of "election." But this interpretation was entirely pragmatic; it was made only because it had to be made, because in the most literal sense one could not survive in a universe of absolute pre-

"The Liberal Conscience in *The Crucible*" by Robert Warshow. From *The Immediate Experience* by Robert Warshow (New York: Doubleday and Company, Inc., 1962). Reprinted by permission of Joseph Goldberg, Trustee of the Estate of Robert Warshow.

destination. The central contradiction of Calvinism remained unresolved, and the awful confusions of the Puritan mind still embarrass our efforts to see the early history of New England as a clear stage in the progress of American enlightenment. Only Hawthorne among American writers has seriously tried to deal with these confusions as part of the "given" material of literature, taking the Puritans in their own terms as among the real possibilities of life, and the admiration we accord to his tense and brittle artistry is almost as distant as our admiration of the early New Englanders themselves; it is curious how rarely Hawthorne has been mentioned beside Melville and James even in recent explorations of the "anti-liberal" side of our literature.

The Salem witch trials represent how far the Puritans were ready to go in taking their doctrines seriously. Leaving aside the slavery question and what has flowed from it, those trials are perhaps the most disconcerting single episode in our history: the occurrence of the unthinkable on American soil, and in what our schools have rather successfully taught us to think of as the very "cradle of Americanism." Of Europe's witch trials, we have our opinion. But these witch trials are "ours"; where do they belong in the "tradition"?

For Americans, a problem of this sort demands to be resolved, and there have been two main ways of resolving it. The first is to regard the trials as a historical curiosity; a curiosity by definition requires no explanation. In this way the trials are placed among the "vagaries" of the Puritan mind and can even offer a kind of amusement, like the amusement we have surprisingly agreed to find in the so-called "rough justice" of the Western frontier in the last century. But the more usual and more deceptive way of dealing with the Salem trials has been to assimilate them to the history of progress in civil rights. This brings them into the world of politics, where, even if our minds are not always made up, at least we think we know what the issues are. Arthur Miller, I need hardly say, has adopted this latter view.

Inevitably, I suppose, we will find in history what we need to find. But in this particular "interpretation" of the facts there seems to be a special injustice. The Salem trials were not political and had nothing whatever to do with civil rights, unless it is a violation of civil rights to hang a murderer. Nor were the "witches" being "persecuted"—as the Puritans did persecute Quakers, for instance. The actual conduct of the trials, to be sure, was outrageous, but no more outrageous than the conduct of ordinary criminal trials in England at the time. In any case,

it is a little absurd to make the whole matter rest on the question of
fair trial: how can there be a "fair trial" for a crime which not only has
not been committed, but is impossible? The Salem "witches" suffered
something that may be worse than persecution: they were hanged because of a metaphysical error. And they chose to die—for all could have
saved themselves by "confession"—not for a cause, not for "civil rights,"
not even to defeat the error that hanged them, but for their own credit
on earth and in heaven: they would not say they were witches when they
were not. They lived in a universe where each man was saved or damned
by himself, and what happened to them was personal. Certainly their
fate is not lacking in universal significance; it was a human fate. But its
universality—if we must have the word—is of that true kind which begins and ends in a time and a place. One need not believe in witches,
or even in God, to understand the events in Salem, but it is mere provin-
ciality to ignore the fact that both those ideas had a reality for the people
of Salem that they do not have for us.

The "universality" of Mr. Miller's play belongs neither to literature
nor to history, but to that journalism of limp erudition which assumes
that events are to be understood by referring them to categories, and
which is therefore never at a loss for a comment. Just as in *Death of a
Salesman* Mr. Miller sought to present "the American" by eliminating so
far as possible the "non-essential" facts which might have made his protagonist a particular American, so in *The Crucible* he reveals at every
turn his almost contemptuous lack of interest in the particularities—
which is to say, the reality—of the Salem trials. The character and motives of all the actors in this drama are for him both simple and clear.
The girls who raised the accusation of witchcraft were merely trying to
cover up their own misbehavior. The Reverend Samuel Parris found in
the investigation of witchcraft a convenient means of consolidating his
shaky position in a parish that was murmuring against his "undemo-
cratic" conduct of the church. The Reverend John Hale, a conscientious
and troubled minister who, given the premises, must have represented
something like the best that Puritan New England had to offer, and
whose agonies of doubt might have been expected to call forth the
highest talents of a serious playwright, appears in *The Crucible* as a kind
of idiotic "liberal" scoutmaster, at first cheerfully confident of his ability
to cope with the Devil's wiles and in the last act babbling hysterically in
an almost comic contrast to the assured dignity of the main characters.
Deputy Governor Danforth, presented as the virtual embodiment of

early New England, never becomes more than a pompous, unimaginative politician of the better sort.

As for the victims themselves, the most significant fact is Miller's choice of John Proctor for his leading character: Proctor can be seen as one of the more "modern" figures in the trials, hardheaded, skeptical, a voice of common sense (he thought the accusing girls could be cured of their "spells" by a sound whipping); also, according to Mr. Miller, no great churchgoer. It is all too easy to make Proctor into the "common man"— and then, of course, we know where we are: Proctor wavers a good deal, fails to understand what is happening, wants only to be left alone with his wife and his farm, considers making a false confession, but in the end goes to his death for reasons that he finds a little hard to define but that are clearly good reasons—mainly, it seems, he does not want to implicate others. You will never learn from this John Proctor that Salem was a religious community, quite as ready to hang a Quaker as a witch. The saintly Rebecca Nurse is also there, to be sure, sketched in rapidly in the background, a quiet figure whose mere presence—there is little more of her than that—reminds us how far the dramatist has fallen short.

Nor has Mr. Miller hesitated to alter the facts to fit his constricted field of vision. Abigail Williams, one of the chief accusers in the trials, was about eleven years old in 1692; Miller makes her a young woman of eighteen or nineteen and invents an adulterous relation between her and John Proctor in order to motivate her denunciation of John and his wife Elizabeth. The point is not that this falsifies the facts of Proctor's life (though one remembers uneasily that he himself was willing to be hanged rather than confess to what was not true), but that it destroys the play, offering an easy theatrical motive that even in theatrical terms explains nothing, and deliberately casting away the element of religious and psychological complexity which gives the Salem trials their dramatic interest in the first place. In a similar way, Miller risks the whole point of *Death of a Salesman* by making his plot turn on the irrelevant discovery of Willy Loman's adultery. And in both plays the fact of adultery itself is slighted: it is brought in not as a human problem, but as a mere theatrical device, like the dropping of a letter; one cannot take an interest in Willy Loman's philandering, or believe in Abigail Williams' passion despite the barnyard analogies with which the playwright tries to make it "elemental."

Mr. Miller's steadfast, one might almost say selfless, refusal of complexity, the assured simplicity of his view of human behavior, may be the chief source of his ability to captivate the educated audience. He is an oddly depersonalized writer; one tries in vain to define his special quality, only to discover that it is perhaps not a quality at all, but something like a method, and even as a method strangely bare: his plays are as neatly put together and essentially as empty as that skeleton of a house which made *Death of a Salesman* so impressively confusing. He is the playwright of an audience that believes the frightening complexities of history and experience are to be met with a few ideas, and yet does not even possess these ideas any longer but can only point significantly at the place where they were last seen and where it is hoped they might still be found to exist. What this audience demands of its artists above all is an intelligent narrowness of mind and vision and a generalized tone of affirmation, offering not any particular insights or any particular truths, but simply the assurance that insight and truth as qualities, the things in themselves, reside somehow in the various signals by which the artist and the audience have learned to recognize each other. For indeed very little remains except this recognition; the marriage of the liberal theater and the liberal audience has been for some time a marriage in name only, held together by habit and mutual interest, partly by sentimental memory, most of all by the fear of loneliness and the outside world; and yet the movements of love are still kept up—for the sake of the children, perhaps.

The hero of this audience is Clifford Odets. Among those who shouted "Bravo!" at the end of *The Crucible*—an exclamation, awkward on American lips, that is reserved for cultural achievements of the greatest importance—there must surely have been some who had stood up to shout "Strike!" at the end of *Waiting for Lefty*. But it is hard to believe that a second Odets, if that were possible, or the old Odets restored to youth, would be greeted with such enthusiasm as Arthur Miller calls forth. Odet's talent was too rich—in my opinion the richest ever to appear in the American theater—and his poetry and invention were constantly more important than what he conceived himself to be saying. In those days it didn't matter: the "message" at the end of the third act was so much taken for granted that there was room for Odet's exuberance, and he himself was never forced to learn how much his talent was superior to his "affirmations" (if he had learned, perhaps the talent might have survived the "affirmations"). Arthur Miller is the dramatist of a later time, when the "message" isn't there at all, but it has been agreed to pretend that it is. This pretense can be maintained only by the most rigid control, for there is no telling what small element of dramatic *élan* or simple reality may destroy the delicate rapport of a theater and an audience that have not yet acknowledged they have no more to say to each other. Arthur Miller is Odets without the poetry. Worst of all, one feels sometimes that he has suppressed the poetry deliberately, making himself by choice the anonymous dramatist of a fossilized audience. In *Death of a Salesman,* certainly, there were moments when reality seemed to force its way momentarily to the surface. And even at *The Crucible* —though here it was not Miller's suppressed talent that broke through, but the suppressed facts of the outside world—the thread that tied the audience to its dramatist must have been now and then under some strain: surely there were some in the audience to notice uneasily that these witch trials, with their quality of ritual and their insistent need for "confessions," were much more like the trial that had just ended in Prague than like any trial that has lately taken place in the United States. So much the better, perhaps, for the play's "universal significance"; I don't suppose Mr. Miller would defend the Prague trial. And yet I cannot believe it was for this particular implication that anyone shouted "Bravo!"

For let us indeed not be misled. Mr. Miller has nothing to say about the Salem trials and makes only the flimsiest pretense that he has. *The Crucible* was written to say something about Alger Hiss and Owen Lattimore, Julius and Ethel Rosenberg, Senator McCarthy, the actors who have lost their jobs on radio and television, in short the whole complex that is spoken of, with a certain lowering of the voice, as the "present atmosphere." And yet not to say anything about that either, but only to suggest that a great deal might be said, oh an infinitely great deal, if it were not that—what? Well, perhaps if it were not that the "present atmosphere" itself makes such plain speaking impossible. As it is, there is nothing for it but to write plays of "universal significance"—and, after all, that's what a serious dramatist is supposed to do anyway.

What, then, *is* Mr. Miller trying to say to us? It's hard to tell. In *The Crucible* innocent people are accused and convicted of witchcraft on the most absurd testimony—in fact, the testimony of those who themselves have meddled in witchcraft and are therefore doubly to be distrusted. Decent citizens who sign petitions attesting to the good character of their accused friends and neighbors are thrown into prison as suspects. Anyone who tries to introduce into court the voice of reason is likely to be held in contempt. One of the accused refuses to plead and is pressed to death.

No one is acquitted; the only way out for the accused is to make false confessions and themselves join the accusers. Seeing all this on the stage, we are free to reflect that something very like these trials has been going on in recent years in the United States. How much like? Mr. Miller does not say. But *very* like, allowing of course for some superficial differences: no one has been pressed to death in recent years, for instance. Still, people have lost their jobs for refusing to say under oath whether or not they are Communists. The essential pattern is the same, isn't it? And when we speak of "universal significance," we mean sticking to the essential pattern, don't we? Mr. Miller is under no obligation to tell us whether he thinks the trial of Alger Hiss, let us say, was a "witch trial"; he is writing about the Salem trials.

Or, again, the play reaches its climax with John and Elizabeth Proctor facing the problem of whether John should save himself from execution by making a false confession; he elects finally to accept death, for his tormentors will not be satisfied with his mere admission of guilt: he would be required to implicate others, thus betraying his innocent friends, and his confession would of course be used to justify the hanging of the other convicted witches in the face of growing community unrest. Now it is very hard to watch this scene without thinking of Julius and Ethel Rosenberg, who might also save their lives by confessing. Does Mr. Miller believe that the only confession possible for them would be a false one, implicating innocent people? Naturally, there is no way for him to let us know; perhaps he was not even thinking of the Rosenbergs at all. How can he be held responsible for what comes into my head while I watch his play? And if I think of the Rosenbergs and somebody else thinks of Alger Hiss, and still another thinks of the Prague trial, doesn't that simply prove all over again that the play has universal significance?

One remembers also, as John Proctor wrestles with his conscience, that a former close associate of Mr. Miller's decided some time ago, no doubt after serious and painful consideration, to tell the truth about his past membership in the Communist party, that he mentioned some others who had been in the party with him, and that he then became known in certain theatrical circles as an "informer" and a "rat." Is it possible that this is what Mr. Miller was thinking about when he came to write his last scene? And is he trying to tell us that no one who has been a member of the Communist party should admit it? Or that if he does admit it he should not implicate anyone else? Or that all such "confessions" may be assumed to be false? If he were trying to tell us any of these

things, perhaps we might have some arguments to raise. But of course he
isn't; he's only writing about the Salem trials, and who wants to maintain that John Proctor was guilty of witchcraft?

But if Mr. Miller isn't saying anything about the Salem trials, and
can't be caught saying anything about anything else, what did the audience think he was saying? That too is hard to tell. A couple of the news-
paper critics wrote about how timely the play was, and then took it back
in the Sunday editions, putting a little more weight on the "universal
significance"; but perhaps they didn't quite take it back as much as they
seemed to want to: the final verdict appeared to be merely that *The Crucible* is not so great a play as *Death of a Salesman*. As for the rest of the
audience, it was clear that they felt themselves to be participating in an
event of great meaning: that is what is meant by "Bravo!" Does "Bravo!"
mean anything else? I think it means: we agree with Arthur Miller; he
has set forth brilliantly and courageously what has been weighing on
all our minds; at last someone has had the courage to answer Senator
McCarthy.

I don't believe this audience was likely to ask itself what it was agree-
ing to. Enough that someone had said something, anything, to dispel for
a couple of hours that undefined but very real sense of frustration which
oppresses these "liberals"—who believe in their innermost being that
salvation comes from saying something, and who yet find themselves
somehow without anything very relevant to say. They tell themselves, of
course, that Senator McCarthy has made it "impossible" to speak; but one
can hardly believe they are satisfied with this explanation. Where are the
heroic voices that will refuse to be stilled?

Well, last season there was *The Male Animal,* a play written twelve
or thirteen years ago about a college professor who gets in trouble for
reading one of Vanzetti's letters to his English composition class. In the
audience at that play one felt also the sense of communal excitement; it
was a little like a secret meeting of early Christians—or even, one might
say, witches—where everything had an extra dimension of meaning experienced only by the communicants. And this year there has been a
revival of *The Children's Hour,* a play of even more universal significance than *The Crucible* since it doesn't have anything to do with any
trials but just shows how people can be hurt by having lies told about
them. But these were old plays, the voices of an older generation. It remained for Arthur Miller to write a new play that really speaks out.

What does he say when he speaks out?

Never mind. He speaks out.

One question remains to be asked. If Mr. Miller was unable to write directly about what he apparently (one can only guess) feels to be going on in American life today, why did he choose the particular evasion of the Salem trials? After all, violations of civil rights have been not infrequent in our history, and the Salem trials have the disadvantage that they must be distorted in order to be fitted into the framework of civil rights in the first place. Why is it just the image of a "witch trial" or a "witch hunt" that best expresses the sense of oppression which weighs on Mr. Miller and those who feel—I do not say think—as he does?

The answer, I would suppose, is precisely that those accused of witchcraft did *not* die for a cause or an idea, that they represented nothing; they were totally innocent, accused of a crime that does not even exist, the arbitrary victims of a fantastic error. Sacco and Vanzetti, for instance, were able to interpret what was happening to them in a way that the Salem victims could not; they knew that they actually stood for certain ideas that were abhorrent to those who were sending them to death. But the men and women hanged in Salem were not upholding witchcraft against the true church; they were upholding their own personal integrity against an insanely mistaken community.

This offers us a revealing glimpse of the way the Communists and their fellow-travelers have come to regard themselves. The picture has a certain pathos. As it becomes increasingly difficult for any sane man of conscience to reconcile an adherence to the Communist party with any conceivable political principles, the Communist—who is still, let us remember, very much a man of conscience—must gradually divest his political allegiance of all actual content, until he stands bare to the now incomprehensible anger of his neighbors. What can they possibly have against him?—he knows quite well that he believes in nothing, certainly that he is no revolutionist; he is only a dissenter-in-general, a type of personality, a man frozen into an attitude.

From this comes the astonishing phenomenon of Communist innocence. It cannot be assumed that the guiltiest of Communist conspirators protesting his entire innocence may not have a certain belief in his own protest. If you say to a Communist that he is a Communist, he is likely to feel himself in the position of a man who has been accused on no evidence of a crime that he has actually committed. He knows that he happens to be a Communist. But he knows also that his opinions and behavior are only the opinions and behavior of a "liberal," a "dissenter."

You are therefore accusing him of being a Communist because he is a liberal, because he is for peace and civil rights and everything good. By some fantastic accident, your accusation happens to be true, but it is *essentially* false.

Consider, for example, how the controversy over the Hiss case reduced itself almost immediately to a question of personality, the "good" Hiss against the "bad" Chambers, with the disturbing evidence of handwriting and typewriters and automobiles somehow beside the point. Alger Hiss, for those who believe him innocent, wears his innocence on his face and his body, in his "essence," whereas Chambers by his own tortured behavior reveals himself as one of the damned. Hiss's innocence, in fact, exists on a plane entirely out of contact with whatever he may have done. Perhaps most of those who take Hiss's "side" believe that he actually did transmit secret documents to Chambers. But they believe also that this act was somehow transmuted into innocence by the inherent virtue of Alger Hiss's being.

In a similar way, there has grown up around figures like Whittaker Chambers, Elizabeth Bentley, and Louis Budenz the falsest of all false issues: the "question" of the ex-Communist. We are asked to consider, not whether these people are telling the truth, or whether their understanding of Communism is correct, but whether in their "essence" as ex-Communists they are not irredeemably given over to falsehood and confusion. (It must be said that some ex-Communists have themselves helped to raise this absurd "question" by depicting Communism as something beyond both error and immorality—a form of utter perdition.)

Or, finally, consider that most mystical element in the Communist propaganda about the Rosenberg case: the claim that Julius and Ethel Rosenberg are being "persecuted" because they have "fought for peace." Since the Rosenbergs had abstained entirely from all political activity of any sort for a number of years before their arrest, it follows that the only thing they could have been doing which a Communist might interpret as "fighting for peace" must have been spying for the Soviet Union; but their being "persecuted" rests precisely on the claim that they are innocent of spying. The main element here, of course, is deliberate falsification. But it must be understood that for most partisans of the Rosenbergs such a falsification raises no problem; all lies and inconsistencies disappear in the enveloping cloud of the unspoken "essential" truth: the Rosenbergs are innocent *because* they are accused; they are innocent, one might say, by definition.

In however inchoate a fashion, those who sat thrilled in the dark theater watching *The Crucible* were celebrating a tradition and a community. No longer could they find any meaning in the cry of "Strike!" or "Revolt!" as they had done in their younger and more "primitive" age; let it be only "Bravo!"—a cry of celebration with no particular content. The important thing was that for a short time they could experience together the sense of their own being, their close community of right-mindedness in the orthodoxy of "dissent." Outside, there waited all kinds of agonizing and concrete problems: were the Rosenbergs actually guilty? was Stalin actually going to persecute the Jews? But in the theater they could know, immediately and confidently, their own innate and inalienable rightness.

The Salem trials are in fact more relevant than Arthur Miller can have suspected. For this community of "dissent," inexorably stripped of all principle and all specific belief, has retreated at last into a kind of extreme Calvinism of its own where political truth ceases to have any real connection with politics but becomes a property of the soul. Apart from all belief and all action, these people are "right" in themselves, and no longer need to prove themselves in the world of experience; the Revolution—or "liberalism," or "dissent"—has entered into them as the grace of God was once conceived to have entered into the "elect," and, like the grace of God, it is given irrevocably. Just as Alger Hiss bears witness to virtue even in his refusal to admit the very act wherein his "virtue" must reside if it resides anywhere, so these bear witness to "dissent" and "progress" in their mere existence.

For the Puritans themselves, the doctrine of absolute election was finally intolerable, and it cannot be believed that this new community of the elect finds its position comfortable. But it has yet to discover that its discomfort, like its "election," comes from within.

The Whole Man and the Real Witch

by Herbert Blau

When Arthur Miller revived the term Social Drama in his preface to
A View from the Bridge, he was tired of the weeping willowiness of our
plays of lyric neurosis. He was also wary of the tougher drama of estrange-
ment, whether elegiac (Beckett) or swollen to grandeur by threat and
malice (Genet)—making the outcast into a principle of being. What he
wants in Social Drama "is the drama of the whole man." In the introduction to the *Collected Plays,* he said he saw something like it in the drama
of Brecht. While he could not agree with his "concept of the human
situation" (meaning his politics, I suppose), he did feel that Brecht was
working "not on the periphery of the contemporary dramatic problem,
but directly upon its center—which is . . . the problem of consciousness." To achieve consciousness, however, one needs to believe in Society.

If it doesn't assume it, the Social Drama is a drama in search of a body
politic. For Miller, a social humanitarian, it comes out of the desire to
make sense of the word "individual" in a mass society, increasingly de-
prived of identity by machines and machine politics and machine values.
It also comes from his rather academic preoccupation with the tragic
form, where self-realization, the quest of the dramatic hero, is prefigured
in the myths and mores of his people. The word "individual," which
once meant "inseparable," now usually means "alienated." What Miller
is after, almost against the evidence of modern experience, is a drama
in which the individual is not an "individual in his own right," but in
relation to universal substance and the polity as a whole.

Both tragic drama and the idea of heroism floundered when personal
right, becoming a mandate, got lost in the press of the crowd. And even
more so when the private life of men became inconsistent with the generally approved definitions of Man. Or when definition floundered in the

"The Whole Man and the Real Witch" by Herbert Blau. From *The Impossible
Theatre* by Herbert Blau (New York: The Macmillan Company, 1964). Reprinted by
permission of The Macmillan Company.

nihilistic possibility of there is nothing either good or bad but thinking makes it so. The classical trilogy of *Oedipus* shows that, after banishment and disgrace, the final resting place of the outcast is within the City limits. With *Hamlet,* however, the slaughters seem more accidental, the spectators more self-conscious, and it is a stranger who supervises the burial and bids the soldiers shoot. From the beginning, Elsinore is less a City than a state of mind. For a dramatist like Beckett, there is no refuge, as there is only the career of the outcast. We live astride the grave; indeed, we are born to it: "Down in the hole, lingeringly, the grave-digger puts on the forceps." Man's quest for resolution in society is the quest of the psychotic in an armed madhouse, going from one lunatic asylum to another. The only refuge is the closed world of the dispossessed Self, divided against itself; not even the "individual in his own right," for we suffer by nature from impossible dependencies and existential drainage, like the bald patch of Tolstoy's Vronsky, who has pride in himself as a social being. ("Why do we go on tormenting ourselves," says Vronsky, "when everything might be arranged so well?") The drama of Krapp is a drama of the bald patch, mulling over old love. In such a drama Law is a fiction, part of the gibberish of Lucky's speech—a matter of chance, mocked by the firm of "Feckham Peckam Fulham and Clapham."

To Miller, Law is as real as Society. A man may exceed its limits, but the Law is confirmed by excess. Even revolt is dedicated to its preservation. And, as opposed to Beckett or Kafka's *The Trial,* there is access to the Law. Unlike Genet, Miller could never celebrate the frightening dominance of illusion and mutability. The power of change remains in the hands of men; it is a matter of will, operating in a social framework.

Nevertheless, Miller, having seen *The Blacks,* talks now of a Theater of Essences and leads us to anticipate a breakthrough. To date, however, he has been laboring the old forms. He tells us that *Death of a Salesman* destroys the boundaries between now and then in "a mobile concurrency of past and present." But though his argument about the richer scene-changing potential of language as compared to the visual images of film has merit, the treatment of Time in *Salesman* (and in his new play *After the Fall*) seems amateurish compared to that of, say, *Marienbad,* with its multiple series of presences, including several conflicting views of the past, various routes to the present (ambiguously there like hallucination), a realized but contradictory future, and even adumbrations of a reality that may, for all we know, only be wished for. If not flashback, we have in *Salesman* the manipulable Time of a radio drama, "as mad as Willy and as abrupt and as suddenly lyrical," but limited by his derangement so that, wherever he may be, we know exactly where we are.

Now, while this lacks the sophisticated confusion of a *nouvelle vague* film, it may be more of a virtue than we care to remember. And something quite valid is being kept alive in the theater by a playwright who insists, while everybody is relishing confusion as a norm, that the function of drama is to search for "a standard of values that will create in man a respect for himself, a real voice in the fate of his society, and, above all, an aim for his life which is neither a private aim for a private life nor one which sets him below the machine that was made to serve him."

It was another play by Miller, striving to achieve this image in a rather conventional form, that had the most resounding influence on our developing audience. Even to this day, a revival of *The Crucible* will take up slack at the box office. Whatever that may be a sign of, in our theater there was no doubt the reign of McCarthy had a lot to do with its initial success. Miller, however, has tried to minimize the immediate parallel: "It was not only the rise of 'McCarthyism' that moved me, but something which seemed more weird and mysterious. It was the fact that a political, objective, knowledgeable campaign from the far Right was capable of creating not only a terror, but a new subjective reality, a veritable mystique which was gradually assuming even a holy resonance."

The mystique was resonating into an even more subtle shape than Miller had imagined. But while it lacked the terrifying impartiality of greater drama, *The Crucible* had nevertheless the vehemence of good social protest. The play was unevenly cast, put into rehearsal in haste (lest somebody take advantage of the release of rights before we did), the director was replaced after about three weeks, but the actors, upon whom the drama makes no special demands, played it with fervor and conviction if not subtlety. And in our program notes we stressed the McCarthy parallel, speaking of guilt by association and Ordeal by Slander.

The production made us a lot of liberal friends. They are all, all honorable men, but while I have signed the same petitions, that friendship in the theater has always been a little unsettling and subsequent plays have borne out my feeling that if we have the same politics, we do not always have it for the same reasons. While the power of mass psychosis is one of the strongest elements in the play, there is a melodrama in the fervency that always made me uncomfortable. When I brought it up, it made others uncomfortable. But I think it behooves us to understand both the appeal and limitations of those forceful drama—one of those which seems effective so long as it is even middlingly well played, and despite its fate on Broadway.

The Puritan community, as Hawthorne knew in *The Scarlet Letter*, is the ideal setting for a realistic narrative of allegorical dimensions. As Miller puts it, drawing on the annals of the Salem trials: "To write a realistic play of that world was already to write in a style beyond contemporary realism." And there is a powerful admonition beyond that in Proctor's final refusal to be *used*. Like Miller before the congressional committee, he will not lend his name to the naming of names. On this level the play has authority, and it serves as an exemplum. Several critics have pointed out that the analogy between witches and Communists is a weak one, for while we believe in retrospect there were no witches, we know in fact there were some Communists, and a few of them were dangerous. (If Miller were another kind of dramatist, he might claim there *were* witches, but we shall come to that in a moment.) Yet as a generalization, the play's argument is worthy; as a warning against "the handing over of conscience," it is urgent; and to the extent his own public life has required it Miller has shown the courage of his convictions beyond most men—and hence has some right to call for it. One might still wish he were more inventive in form, but in a period where the borders between art and anarchy are ill-defined, we might apply the caution stated in II Corinthians: "All things are lawful, but not all things edify." It is no small thing to say *The Crucible* is an edifying drama.

What the play does not render, however, is what Miller claims for it and what is deeply brooding in the Puritan setting: "the interior psychological question," the harrowing descent of mass hallucination into the life of the individual, where value is deranged, no reason is right, and every man drives his bargain with the sinister. One sees this in *The Brothers Karamazov*, which Miller invokes as that "great book of wonder," and more relevantly in *The Possessed*, where political evil is the reptilian shadow of indecipherable sin. For Proctor, a sin is *arranged*, so that his guilt might have cause. All we can say is: that is not the way it is. For Miller, a psychosis is no more than a psychosis, with clear motive and rational geography. The symptoms are fully describable. His love of wonder is deflated by his desire "to write rationally" and to put a judgmental finger on "the full loathesomeness of . . . anti-social action." The desire is admirable, but the danger is to locate it in advance. Studying Dostoyevsky, Miller had resolved to "let wonder rise up like a mist, a gas, a vapor from the gradual and remorseless crush of factual and psychological conflict." But while that is a good description of the source of wonder in Dostoyevsky, Miller is restive in the mist, which in Dostoyevsky is thickened to nightmare by every wincing judgment and every laceration of meaning, writhing in the imminence of wrong.

By contrast, we know only too well what *The Crucible* means, nor were the issues really ever in doubt. Wanting to write a drama "that would lift out of the morass of subjectivism the squirming, single, defined process" by which public terror unmans us, Miller fills in the record with the adultery of John Proctor and Abigail Williams. He thus provides the rationalist's missing link to the mystery of the crying out. The adultery brings the drama back toward the "subjectivism" Miller was trying to avoid, but its real subjective life remains shallow. Taking up charges of coldness, he says he had never written more passionately and blames the American theater—actors, directors, audience, and critics—for being trained "to take to heart anything that does not prick the mind and to suspect everything that does not supinely reassure."

About the American theater, I think this is exactly so. But my own reservations have to do with the fact that, while moral instruction may be a legitimate ambition of the drama, the play *does* reassure—and it is the *mind* which rebels finally against its formulas while the emotions may be overwhelmed by its force. A play is privileged to reconstruct history for its own purposes; but here we have a play which pretends to describe in realistic terms a community instinctively bent on devotion to God. The Puritans were readers of signs, and the signs, in daily behavior, were evidences of God's will. Hawthorne's novel retains the impermeable quality of that experience by accepting completely the terms of the divine or demonic game. It is yours to choose whose game it really is, according to his strategy of alternative possibilities. But Miller's play makes the choices for you, and its hero does not stand—as one approving critic has said—"foursquare in his own time and place." The records do show that he considered the inquisition a fraud; but though he is bound to the community as a farmer, he does not, in Miller's play, take to heart "all the complex tensions of the Salem community," for he responds to things like an eighteenth century rationalist with little stake in established doctrine. Truer to time and place is the Reverend Hale, who knew "the devil is precise" and saw him in the godly, in himself. He is certainly the more dramatic figure in being compelled to disavow what by instinct and conditioning he has come to believe. Hale resembles Captain Vere in Melville's *Billy Budd,* where the drama is truly divested of "subjectivism" by characters who are, by *allegiance* to retarded doctrine, impaled upon the cross of choice.

One can also see in Melville's Claggart the kind of character that Miller now wishes he had portrayed in Danforth: evil embodied to the utmost, a man so dedicated to evil that by his nature we might know good. Melville saw that to create such a character he would have to stretch his skepticism toward the ancient doctrine of "depravity according to nature," which alone could explain a Claggart or an Iago. He does this by a strategy of insinuation. He suggests to us that there was once such a doctrine, in which intelligent modern men, of course, can hardly believe. The story virtually drives us back to the "superstition," as Kafka virtually restores Original Sin. (I should add that Melville does this in the prose style of the novelette, which could not always be compensated for in the admirable dramatization by Coxe and Chapman.) Doing so, he takes us back through time, justifying as far as form can reach the eternal intimations of Billy's rosy-dawned execution; a scene which is almost enough to make you believe, with the sailors, that a chip of the dockyard boom "was a piece of the Cross."

Almost. Having proposed to us a possibility just over the edge of reason, Melville writes an ironic coda in which he leaves us to take our own risks of interpretation. Miller, for all his moral conviction and belief in free choice, leaves us none. A master of conventional dramaturgy, with all the skills of building and pacing, he drives past the turbid aspect of social hypnosis to the predetermined heroism of Proctor. Perception yields to sensation and the choice of classical tragedy to its wish-fulfillment. (It is curious that Billy, *typed* down to his stammer, is a more inscrutable character than anyone in Miller's play.) The final irony is that John Proctor, dramatic hero of the populist mind, might even be applauded by members of the congressional committee that cited Miller for contempt. It is no accident, too, that in temperament and general conduct Proctor resembles our true culture hero, John Glenn, who would be perfectly cast for the role if the astronauts were to start a little theater. One may not have the courage to be a Proctor at the final drumroll, nor a Glenn at the countdown, but no one doubts they are worthy of imitation.

This absence of doubt reduced the import of *The Crucible* for those who thought about it, while increasing the impact for those who didn't. You do a play for its virtues, and one devious aspect of the art of theater lies in concealing the faults. Actually, my belief is that if you know what's not there, you can deal more powerfully with what is. Little of what I have said, however, came up during rehearsals of *The Crucible* (which was not so much conceived as put on), but rather in critiques and discussions of plays done later. Whatever its weaknesses, the production was hard-driving in keeping with the play's rhythm, and performance by performance the actors rose to overwhelming approval. Because we would be doing better productions which would not be so approved, it was important to keep our heads. And, indeed, I think this attitude has made it more possible for our actors to sustain their belief through more subtle plays that have not been so vigorously applauded.

At the time we produced *The Crucible,* Miller was already the most powerful rational voice in the American theater. Questioning the play later, I wanted the company to understand that to criticize him was to take his ideas seriously, and to begin to give some shape to our own. The people we often had to question most were those with whom we seemed to agree. Because we were all vulnerable to easy judgments and that depth psychology of the surface which is so inherent in American drama (and acting), it was necessary to see why *The Crucible* was not really the "tough" play that Miller claimed; I mean dramatically tough, tough in soul, driving below its partisanship to a judgment of anti-social action from which, as in Dostoyevsky, none of us could feel exempt. I wouldn't have asked the questions if Miller didn't prompt them with his reflections on Social Drama and the tragic form. But compare the action of Proctor to that of the tragic figures of any age—Macbeth, or Brittanicus, or Raskolnikov: can you approve or disapprove of their action? Can you make the choice of imitating them? Or avoid it? *The Crucible* may confirm what we like to think we believe, but it is not, as Miller says, intimidating to an "Anglo-Saxon audience" (or actors), nor does it really shock us into recognizing that we don't believe what we say we do. Beyond that, the profoundest dramas shake up our beliefs, rock our world; in *The Crucible,* our principles are neither jeopardized nor extended, however much we may fail to live by them anyhow.

As for the inquisitors, Miller wants us to see evil naked and unmitigated. I am prepared to believe it exists (I am certain it exists), and I won't even ask where it comes from. But—to be truer than tough—if you want absolute evil, you've got to think more about witches. Miller wants the Puritan community without Puritan premises or Puritan intuitions (which is one reason why, when he appropriates the language, his own suffers in comparison). His liberalism is the kind that, really believing we have outlived the past, thinks it is there to be used. The past just doesn't lie around like that. And one of these days the American theater is really going to have to come to terms with American history.

Axiom for liberals: no play is deeper than its witches.

Arthur Miller's Shifting Image of Man

by Gerald Weales

And the Lord said unto Moses in Midian, Go, return into Egypt.

In 1964, after an eight-years exile in a Midian a great deal less comfortable than that of Moses, Arthur Miller returned to the New York stage. Within a year, he and the Lincoln Center Repertory Theater offered two new plays—*After the Fall* and *Incident at Vichy*. The first of these is an excessively long self-analysis by a character whose biography so much resembles the playwright's that most critics take it as Miller's *Long Day's Journey into Night*. The second is a kind of round-table discussion over a grave, an incident—as the title says—in which one man finds the power to act. Although they are very different in superficial ways, the plays are alike in theme and tone. It is the second of these—the tone— which justifies the biblical quotation with which I have opened this essay. Miller has returned to the stage dressed in prophetic robes, clothed in a ponderousness that his early plays usually escaped. It is as though he came back not as *a* playwright, but as *The* Playwright—with a capital letter, an image of eminence, a sense of his own high seriousness and his duty as an artist. But this is being unfair to the new Miller. He has always taken himself seriously as an artist, and he has always taken seriously the artist's function in society. If the new plays are inferior to the early ones —and I think they are—their shortcomings can best be seen in recognizing that there is not a complete break between early and late Miller. There are similarities in idea, in technique, in language. To understand what is new in the most recent Miller, it is best to look at his work as a

"Arthur Miller's Shifting Image of Man" by Gerald Weales. From *The American Theatre Today* edited by Alan S. Downer (New York: Basic Books, Inc., 1967). Reprinted by permission of Gerald Weales and Basic Books, Inc.

whole, to attempt to understand what he has wanted to say and how he has tried to say it from the beginning.

Compared with most American playwrights, Miller has written a great deal about his work and how it is to be taken. If his speeches, essays, and introductions were collected, they might look skimpy alongside Bertolt Brecht's theoretical writings, but they would form a respectable volume—one, incidentally, in which aesthetics would share space with apologetics and insight would elbow obscurity. Among the most important of his essays is the one called "On Social Plays," which served as an introduction to the 1955 edition of *A View from the Bridge*. Although there is a kind of vagueness about the essay, as there is about so much of Miller's critical writing, it does make clear that he believes that the serious playwright must write social drama. For him, however, the genre is not simply "an arraignment of society's evils." The true social drama, which he calls the "Whole Drama," must recognize that man has both a subjective and an objective existence, that he belongs not only to himself and his family but to the world beyond. This definition fits the four plays that made Miller famous—*All My Sons* (1947), *Death of a Salesman* (1949), *The Crucible* (1953), and *A View from the Bridge* (1955). With a shift in emphasis, it also fits the two plays produced in 1964.

If a playwright is to be concerned with both psychological man and social man, as Miller's definition of social drama says he must, he is inevitably forced to deal with the problem of identity. This is what Miller has always written about, and it is as clearly the subject of *Incident at Vichy* as it is of *All My Sons*. In Miller's early work, each of his heroes is involved in a struggle which results from his acceptance or his rejection of an image of himself—an image that grows out of the values and the prejudices of his society. That society may be as narrow as Eddie Carbone's neighborhood in *A View from the Bridge* or as wide as the contemporary America that helped form the Willy Loman we meet in *Death of a Salesman*. Although this preoccupation may be found in most of Miller's short stories, in his novel *Focus,* and in his very early plays, it can be seen most clearly where it is most effectively presented—in his major plays, beginning with *All My Sons*. The hero of that play, Joe Keller, is a case in point. He is a good husband and a good father, but he fails to be the good man, the good citizen that his son Chris demands. Near the end of the play, Joe cries out: "I'm his father and he's my son, and if there's something bigger than that I'll put a bullet in my head!" When Chris, now dead, convinces him through a letter that there is something bigger, that his guilt in shipping out faulty airplane parts cannot be excused by his desire to save the family business, Joe does commit suicide. His death, however, is more than a single man's punishment, for Joe Keller is a product of his society. He not only accepts the American myth of the privacy of the family, but he has adopted as a working instrument the familiar attitude that there is a difference between morality and business ethics. Joe Keller is a self-made man, an image of American success, who is destroyed when he is forced to see that image in another context—through the eyes of his idealist son.

After the narrow didacticism of *All My Sons,* Miller went on to write, in *Death of a Salesman,* a play in which the social implications are so firmly enmeshed in the psychological make-up of his hero that it is never possible to reduce Willy's pathetic death to social criticism. When we meet Willy, he, like Joe Keller, is past the point of choice. From the conflicting success images that wander through his troubled brain comes Willy's double ambition—to be rich and to be loved. As he tells Ben: "the wonder of this country [is] that a man can end with diamonds here on the basis of being liked!" Willy's faith in the magic of "personal attractiveness" as a way to success carries him beyond cause and effect to necessity; he assumes that success falls inevitably to the man with the right smile, the best line, the most charm—the man who is not only liked, but "well liked." He has completely embraced the American myth, born of the advertisers, that promises us love and a fortune as soon as we clear up our pimples, stop underarm perspiration, learn to play the piano; for this reason, the brand names that turn up in Willy's speeches are more than narrow realism. He regularly confuses labels with reality. In his last scene with his son Biff, Willy cries out: "I am not a dime a dozen! I am Willy Loman, and you are Biff Loman!" The strength and the pathos of that cry lie in the fact that Willy still thinks that the name should mean something; it is effective within the play because we have heard him imply that a punching bag is good because, as he says, "It's got Gene Tunney's signature on it."

The distance between the actual Willy and the Willy as image is so great when the play opens that he can no longer lie to himself with conviction; what the play gives us is the final disintegration of a man who has never even approached his idea of what by rights he ought to have been. His ideal may have been the old salesman, who at the age of eighty-four could, through the strength of personality, sit in a hotel room and command buyers; but his model is that American mythic figure, the traveling salesman of the dirty joke. Willy shares his culture's conviction that personality is a matter of mannerism and in the sharing develops a style that is compounded of falseness, the mock assurance of what his son Happy calls "the old humor, the old confidence." His act, however, is as much for himself as it is for his customers. The play shows quite clearly that from the beginning of his career Willy has lied about the size of his sales, the warmth of his reception, the number of his friends. It is true that he occasionally doubts himself, but usually he rationalizes his failure. His continuing self-delusion and his occasional self-awareness serve the same purpose; they keep him from questioning the assumptions that lie beneath his failure and his pretense of success.

By the time we get to him, his struggle to hold on to his dream has become so intense that all control is gone. Past and present have become one, and so have fact and fiction. When Biff tries to give him peace by making him realize that there is no crime in being a failure and a mediocrity, Willy hears only what he wants to hear. He takes Biff's tears not only as an evidence of love, which they are, but as a kind of testimonial, an assurance that Willy's way has been the right one all along. Once again secure in his dream, Willy goes to his suicide's death, convinced that when Biff gets the insurance money, "that boy is going to be magnificent." The play is not a simple rejection of Willy's dream. Since Willy has spent his life trying to fit himself into one of the pigeonholes of our society and since Biff is so much like Willy, the final irony of the play may lie in Biff's end-of-the-play declaration, "I know who I am, kid."

Joe Keller and Willy Loman are both consenting victims, men who attach themselves to images which their society has created and called good. The hero of Miller's next play, *The Crucible,* refuses to accept the label that his society tries to force on him. John Proctor dies at the end— and his society kills him—but his death is a romantic one, a kind of triumph, an affirmation of the individual. It may be that Proctor's decision to hang rather than to confess grew out of Miller's involvement in the immediate political situation from which *The Crucible* was drawn. It was the McCarthy era, when so many writers and performers—moved by fear or economic necessity or a genuine break with their ideological past—stepped forward to confess their political sins and to name their fellow sinners. Under such circumstances, it is hardly surprising that Miller chose a hero who could say *no.* And yet the playwright was not interested in a simple propaganda play.

The materials for such a play are there—the hysteria-ridden community, the corrupt accusers, the innocent good people willing to die for their principles. With John Proctor, however, Miller goes for something deeper than the one-dimensional "good guy." Proctor is enough a product of his society to think of himself as a sinner for having slept with Abigail Williams; so he carries a burden of guilt before he is charged with having consorted with the devil. When he is finally faced with the choice of death or confession, his guilt as an adulterer becomes confused with his innocence as a witch; one sin against society comes to look like another. The stage is set for another victim-hero, for a John Proctor who is willing to be what men say he is, but at the last minute he chooses to be his own man. "How may I live without my name?" he asks and, finding no answer, he tears up his confession and goes to the gallows.

Eddie Carbone in *A View from the Bridge* also dies crying out for his name, but he is asking for a lie that will let him live or, failing that, for death. Eddie is like Joe Keller and Willy Loman in that he accepts the rules of his society, an Italian neighborhood in Brooklyn, but he dies because he violates them. Miller wants us to believe that Eddie informs on Rodolpho, an illegal immigrant, because he is driven by a passion as powerful and as impersonal as fate. The interesting thing about Eddie is not the passion that pushes him, but his refusal to recognize it for what it is. He gets rid of Rodolpho not so much out of jealousy, but because the boy's presence nags at him, almost forces him to put a label on his incestuous love for his niece and his homosexual attraction to the boy himself. It is almost as though he becomes an *informer* to keep from wearing some name still more terrible to him. He cannot live under the lesser label either, so he moves into battle with the avenging brother Marco, demanding, "Gimme my name."

Each of these plays has a personality of its own, an action and an intention that separates it from the other three, but all of them are variations on the same theme. The basic premise of all four is that society is an image-making machine, a purveyor of myths and prejudices which provide the false faces and false values which modern man wears. The implication is that the individual has little choice—that he can conform and be destroyed, as Joe Keller and Willy Loman are, or that he can refuse to conform and be destroyed, as John Proctor and Eddie Carbone are. Despite the blackness of this description, the plays are not pessimistic, because inherent in them is a kind of vague faith in man, a suspicion that the individual may finally be able to retain his integrity. This possibility appears, most conventionally, in the platitudes of Chris, the avenging idealist of *All My Sons,* and in the kind of death John Proctor dies in *The Crucible.* In *A View from the Bridge* it lies outside the action of the play, in Miller's attempt, speaking through the narrator Alfieri, to engraft a ritual purity on Eddie: "not purely good, but himself purely."

If the possibility appears at all in *Death of a Salesman*—and I think it does—it does not lie in the possible right choice implied by Biff's "He had the wrong dreams." It certainly does not lie in Biff himself, in all those references to working with the hands, nor in the alternative suggested by Charley and Bernard. It is in Willy's vitality, in his perverse commitment to a pointless dream, in his inability simply to walk away. This last phrase, of course, is a paraphrase of one of Miller's unnecessary attempts to define tragedy. What I'm saying about *Death of a Salesman,* I suppose, is that Willy Loman is a character so complex, so contradictory, so vulnerable, so insensitive, so trusting, so distrustful, so blind, so aware—in short, so human—that he forces man on us by being one.

A few years after these plays were written, Miller tried to give a positive name to whatever it was in man that was going to save him. He had tried before in *Situation Normal,* the book he wrote during the war, but the best he could come up with then was: "And that Belief says, simply, that we believe all men are equal." In the late 1950's he succumbed to the bromide of the decade and began to talk about love. In the introduction to the *Collected Plays,* he added an ex-post-facto alternative to *Death of a Salesman* by suggesting that Biff represents a "system of love" that can oppose Willy's "law of success." In "Bridge to a Savage World," an *Esquire* article containing material that was to go into a film on juvenile delinquency, Miller speaks of "the measure of love which we must bring to our lives if we are not to slide back into a life of violence." [1] Finally, in *The Misfits,* his 1961 film, he lets his hero and heroine, like a William Inge couple, follow "that big star straight on" to find their way home in the dark. Brotherhood and love, however admirable, are a bit amorphous divorced from a specific doctrine—religious, political, or psychological. The terms might have some meaning in a particular situation (if it is not a literary cliché, like the end of *The Misfits*), but it is always difficult to extrapolate from a momentary experience to find a general principle by which man can live. That I assume

[1] Arthur Miller, "Bridge to a Savage World," *Esquire,* October 1958, 185–90.

is what Quentin means in *After the Fall* when he says forlornly: "Social-ism once, then love; some final hope is gone that always saved before the end!"

Despite Quentin's statement of loss, *After the Fall* ends in a positive act, and so does *Incident at Vichy*. Quentin goes to meet Holga, ready to commit himself once again to a personal relationship—which we are to take as a commitment to life. The Prince in *Incident at Vichy* gives up the pass that would free him to save Leduc's life. Despite these acts, however, the two new plays are a great deal more somber than the early Miller plays. The difference is a philosophic one, or would be if the early plays were as formal in their point of view as the new ones are. The difference lies in the way Miller uses the problem of identity. I do not mean that he has ceased to accept that men have images forced upon them. One of the lines of action in *Incident at Vichy*—although it might be called *a line of inaction*—has to do with the failure of the waiting men to resist what is being done to them. A great deal of the discussion has to do with how one should act in the face of his destroyers, what role he should play in an attempt to save himself. The implication is that their failure to agree to attack the guard is their way of consenting to their own destruction. Lebeau, the painter, admits that he feels guilty although he knows he has done nothing wrong and he is not ashamed of being a Jew. Yet, he can say: "Maybe it's that they keep saying such terrible things about us, and you can't answer." It is Leduc, the psy-chiatrist, who states the proposition formally: "So that one way or the other, with illusions or without them, exhausted or fresh—we have been trained to die." Although there is a relationship between this kind of thinking and the conception of Willy Loman as a man attempting to be the success his society admires, there is a great difference too. Willy, as a consenting victim, is a product of Miller's observation; the consenting victims of *Incident at Vichy* are products turned out on the Bruno Bettelheim–Hannah Arendt line—explanations of totalitarian success which almost become apologies for it.

There is, then, a qualitative difference between the conceptions of society in *Death of a Salesman* and in *Incident at Vichy*. That difference, however, is not apparent if we look at *After the Fall* alongside *Salesman*. The pressures that beset Quentin and his friends and relatives are not necessarily the same ones that push Willy around, but they are the same kind. It is clear in *After the Fall* that much of Maggie's behavior is the result of her doing what is expected of her, and that Louise sees herself and Quentin in the roles that her psychoanalysis insists that they play. In the political subplot, Mickey testifies and names names partly because his new affluence requires that he should, and Lou, who makes a John Proctor-refusal, admits that in the past he has compromised his sense of his own honesty, tailored himself to fit Party requirements.

Yet *After the Fall* and *Incident at Vichy* are thematically two of a kind. The real split between these two plays and the earlier ones can be found in what the heroes are looking for—or, at least, in what they find. Like John Proctor and Eddie Carbone, both Quentin and Von Berg are concerned about their names. When Leduc seems surprised that Von Berg should take his title seriously, the Prince answers: "It is not a 'title'; it is my name, my family." Since he goes on to use words like *dishonor,* one might assume that *name* has the same value here as it does in *A View from the Bridge* or *The Crucible.* At this point in the play, it may have such value, at least for Von Berg, but the lesson that the play is going to teach him is to understand *name* as Quentin uses it when he keeps asking over and over in whose name one turns one's back. In the early Miller plays the quest for identity, for name, was a search for integrity. In *After the Fall* and *Incident at Vichy* that quest has become an attempt to find a workable definition.

In *After the Fall,* Quentin is faced with the problem of coming to some conclusion about himself which will make it possible for him to operate in the world. He is attracted to Holga, but he hesitates to commit himself to her, because so many of the commitments of his past—personal, political, and professional—have collapsed, leaving him nothing. The play is Quentin's look at that past, his attempt to find meaning in it. Early in the play, he says sadly: "I feel . . . unblessed." He is bothered throughout the play by a girl named Felice, whom he cannot get out of his mind. Once, casually, he did something that changed the course of her life, and he continually sees her, her hand lifted in benediction, saying: "I'll always bless you." At the end of the play, when he faces the figures from his past, like the director in Fellini's *8½,* he stops Felice from lifting her hand. He accepts that he is unblessed. What he learns in the course of the play is that he has spent his life trying, one way or another, to establish his innocence. The guilt that he feels about the way he has treated his family, about his two failed marriages, about his reluctance to defend his old friend has always been transferred to the other person in the relationship. At the end, he accepts that it is after the fall, that there is no innocence, that the guilt is his. Earlier in the play Holga tells him her recurrent dream. In it she has an idiot child, which she knows represents her life; she wants to run away from it, but she stays and finally she brings herself to kiss it. In case Quentin or the audience has missed the point of the dream, she adds the moral: "I think one must finally take one's life in one's arms, Quentin."

Accepting one's life—at least in the context of *After the Fall*—is more complicated than simply recognizing that any relationship implies responsibilities on both sides. The guilt that Quentin assumes is something very like original sin: an acceptance that he—and all men—are evil. Or that they have evil in them—the capacity to kill. This is presented several ways in the play. Verbally, in Quentin's statements about his failure to grieve for his dead—for Lou, for his mother, for Maggie—visually, in the scene in which he begins to strangle Maggie and finds himself strangling his mother; metaphorically, in the concentration-camp tower that broods over the whole play. This is the element in the play that is most difficult to take, but it is a necessary part of the idea Miller has imposed on his play. Toward the end of the play, Quentin turns toward the tower and says: "My brothers died here . . ." and then, looking down at Maggie lying at his feet, goes on ". . . but my brothers built this place." What is finally being said in *After the Fall* is not that Quentin's life shows him capable of cruelty, of murder even, but that he must accept his complicity in all the evil in the world. Holga, who carries the messages for Miller, says: ". . . no one they didn't kill can be innocent again."

Incident at Vichy comes to the same conclusion. In this instance it is not self-examination that brings self-knowledge to Von Berg; it is a lesson forced on him from outside by Leduc, who from the beginning of the play has accepted that man is inherently evil. When he remarks that he believes the rumor that there are furnaces waiting to destroy them all, it is not because the destroyers are Germans or Nazis, but "It's exactly because they are people that I speak this way." Von Berg, on the other hand, believes that there are "certain people," not identifiable by race or class, through whom all that is best in civilization will finally survive. He imagines that his sympathy for the suffering of the Jews separates him from their tormentors. He is so horrified by what has happened in his native Austria that he has, as he says, "put a pistol to my head!" But he has not pulled the trigger and, as Holga points out in *After the Fall*, by being alive he fails to be innocent. Leduc reminds him that the cousin he mentions early in the play, a man for whom he obviously has some affection, is a Nazi. "It's not your guilt I want," says Leduc, "it's your responsibility."

That statement, however, is false—if not for Leduc, certainly for Miller. What he wants in this play is for Von Berg to recognize his guilt, as Quentin accepts his in *After the Fall*. In an article in *The New York Times Magazine*[2] Miller set out to correct some misconceptions that he felt had grown up around *Incident at Vichy*. He makes quite clear that, to him, the story is relatively unimportant and that Von Berg's heroic act at the end is gratuitous. "The first problem is not what to do about it," he says, "but to discover our own relationship to evil, its reflection of ourselves." If Quentin is a usable analogy for Miller himself, it would seem that the events of the eight years before the writing of *Vichy* made Miller find in himself qualities that he can accept only with difficulty. The accepting becomes possible, however, by extending the *mea culpa* to take in all men. He chooses to do this by embracing the common-places of contemporary psychology, but—since he is still a social dramatist —he uses the complicity gambit to turn personal guilt into public guilt. What this means to Miller as a playwright is that he no longer deals with man's struggle against the images being forced on him; instead, he becomes an image-forcer himself. After all the identity searching, the name that Quentin and Von Berg end up with is Everyman as Execu-tioner. Both plays suggest—insist really—that once this label is accepted, once the illusion of innocence is pushed aside, a man is free to act—even to act as a lover (like Quentin) or a martyr (like Von Berg). These posi-tive acts, however, are simply the residue left by the burning away of the naïve belief in man implicit in the early plays. In *After the Fall* and *Incident at Vichy,* the heroes are not in a struggle; they are in analysis. The analysis is successful when they accept that they fit the love-hate stereotype of the psychological man.

At the beginning of this chapter, I said that *Fall* and *Vichy* are inferior to the earlier plays. Although what Miller has to say in the new plays is philosophically suspect, it is not his theme but his commitment to it that has crippled his work. His new truth is not an impetus to creativity, but a doctrine that must be illustrated. In the past, he has occasionally been criticized for his didacticism, but in none of the early plays, not even in *All My Sons* and *The Crucible,* has he sacrificed action to argu-

[2] Arthur Miller, "Our Guilt for the World's Evil," *The New York Times Magazine,* January 3, 1965, pp. 10–11, 48.

ment. There are defects enough in the early plays—the hidden-letter trick in *All My Sons,* Elizabeth's loving lie in *The Crucible*—defects that grow out of a need to let the action make a social point. Still, his main characters—even John Proctor—are more than one-dimensional vehicles. All the early plays are attempts to understand man and his society by confronting a particular man with a particular situation. The generalizations to be made from that particularity lie outside the play—with the audience, with the critic, with the playwright in his theoretical writings. In the new plays, the situations and the characters are only demonstration models. The playwright has moved from the creation of character to the making of statements, from the concrete to the abstract. This can best be seen if we look at *After the Fall* alongside *Death of a Salesman,* the early play that it most resembles.

The first title for *Salesman* was *The Inside of His Head,* which would suit *After the Fall* just as well. According to the first stage direction of *Fall:* "The action takes place in the mind, thought, and memory of Quentin." Although the version of *Salesman* that finally reached the stage has objective scenes as well as subjective ones, both *Salesman* and *After the Fall* make use of the ideas and the devices of expressionistic theater. The barriers of time and space disappear. The skeletal set of *Salesman* and the free-form set of *Fall* were conceived to let Miller's heroes step freely from the present to the past, or, particularly in the case of Quentin, from one moment in the past to another. Both plays are designed, then, to let the playwright (and his characters) escape the restrictions of conventional realism. The difference between the two plays lies in the way the playwright uses his freedom. In *Salesman* we follow Willy through the last desperate day of his existence, watching him clutch at impossible and mostly imaginary straws, until, through Biff, he is able to find the release that will let him die. The jumble of memories that nag at him are not simply explanatory flashbacks, although there is exposition in them. Since they are as real to Willy as the immediate events, they contribute to his disintegration. In *Salesman,* then, all the scenes are part of the play's action. In *After the Fall* this is hardly the case. What happens in that play is that Quentin decides to go meet Holga at the airport; the action, presumably, is his process of reaching that decision. When we meet him at the beginning of the play he is somewhat worried by the fact that hope keeps sneaking up on him even though he knows how awful everything is. The play uses his life to explain to him that he is the psychological stereotype I discussed above. Then, perversely hopeful in a terrible world full of potential killers like himself, he goes off to meet the girl. Although there are lines to suggest that Quentin is undergoing some kind of torment, the pain of his self-analysis is belied by the discursive, man-to-man stance which he takes during the narrative sections of the play. The remembered scenes, then, do not have the look of experiences being undergone, but of illustrations to prove a point. Even if we were to believe that Quentin is actually coming to conclusions as we watch him, those conclusions—his acceptance of himself—do not lead logically nor dramatically to Holga. It is as though he stepped to the front of the stage and said: "I have a few hours to kill before I meet a plane. Let me spend it describing the human condition."

In *Incident at Vichy* there is the same kind of disconnection between the lesson Von Berg learns and his decision to die for Leduc. Some time ago in *The New York Times* David Ross, reviewing a number of his fellow poets, said of one that she had fallen prey to "the thematic fallacy, the idea that lofty subjects are what make great poetry." [3] Miller seems to be suffering from the same fallacy in *After the Fall* and *Incident at Vichy*.

The disappointment that many of us feel at the new plays should not be taken as a condemnation of Miller's work. He is still one of our most important playwrights, with three good plays and one extremely fine one to his credit. To have written *Death of a Salesman* is an achievement of such significance that Arthur Miller can be allowed a slip, or even a *Fall*.

[3] David Ross, "A Matter of Image," *The New York Times Book Review*, February 21, 1965, p. 4.

Arthur Miller's Later Plays

by Harold Clurman

I. ARTHUR MILLER: THEME AND VARIATIONS

After the Fall, the opening production of the Repertory Theater of Lincoln Center, is Arthur Miller's first play in nine years. It offers us a vantage point from which to examine the man and his work. It is a bridge from which we may look backward to his starting point and forward to the way ahead.

When recently asked in what way his plays were related to the events of his life Miller replied, "In a sense all my plays are autobiographical." The artist creates his biography through his work even as the events of his life serve to shape him.

He was born on One Hundred Twelfth Street in Manhattan in 1915. He is one of three children. He has an elder brother in business, a sister on the stage. The Millers were unequivocally middle-class and Jewish. His mother, no longer living, was born in the United States; his father, a manufacturer of women's coats, was born in what before the First World War was part of the Austro-Hungarian empire. Till the Depression of the Thirties the Millers were a moderately well-to-do family. Arthur attended grammar school in Harlem and went to high school in Brooklyn.

By the time he finished high school Arthur's parents could no longer afford to send him to college. His grades were not sufficiently high to qualify him for entry into the school of his choice, the University of Michigan. He found two ways out of this dilemma. He got himself a job in a warehouse on Tenth Avenue and Sixtieth Street as a "loader"

"Arthur Miller's Later Plays" (editor's title), comprises three articles by Harold Clurman which were originally published separately: "Arthur Miller: Theme and Variations" from *Theatre I* (New York: Hill and Wang, Inc., 1964); "Director's Notes: *Incident at Vichy*" from *Tulane Drama Review,* IX, No. 4 (1965), 77–90; and "The Merits of Mr. Miller," © 1968 by The New York Times Company, from *The New York Times,* April 21, 1968, II, pp. 1 and 3. All are reprinted by permission of Harold Clurman and the publishers.

and shipping clerk. He saved a sum sufficient to pay his tuition. He also wrote a letter to the President of the University and asked for a chance to prove his merit within the first year of his studies. If he failed to distinguish himself he would quit. He did very well and stayed on to take his degree of Bachelor of Arts.

In his boyhood Arthur was neither particularly bright nor very well read. He was a baseball fan. He began to read while working at the warehouse. He is probably the only man who ever read through *War and Peace* entirely on the subway, standing up. At college he also began to write—plays. Several of them were awarded the Jule and Avery Hopwood prize of the University of Michigan. One of them won a prize of $1,250 given by the Theatre Guild's Bureau of New Plays. With money from these prizes and $22.77 a week from the Federal Theatre Project, Miller was able to support himself during the early years of his career. He was living at Patchogue, Long Island, at the time and had to check in every day at the Project office in Manhattan to collect his wage. He wrote a play about Montezuma which was submitted to the Group Theatre, as well as to others, no doubt, and which the author of the present article, then the Group Theatre's Managing Director, found several years later in his files—unread!

In 1944 while visiting various army camps in the United States, a diary Miller kept as research for a film, *The Story of G.I. Joe* (the war life of Ernie Pyle), was published under the title, *Situation Normal*. In 1945, as a reaction to the activities of a Fascist organization known as the Christian Front, Miller wrote his only novel, *Focus*, which attracted considerable attention. Its subject was anti-semitism.

That year saw the production of Miller's first play, *The Man Who Had All the Luck*, which had no luck at all: there were only four performances. Still Miller was launched! One critic, Burton Rascoe, recognized a potentially powerful playwright. More important, several producers including the present writer got in touch with Miller requesting him to submit his next play. That was *All My Sons* which was produced by Harold Clurman, Elia Kazan and Walter Fried on January 29, 1947. It was a box-office success and was voted the Best Play of the Season by the Drama Critics' Circle.

In recounting the bare facts of his background Miller remarked in passing that in the Presidential campaign of 1932 he favored the Republican candidate. Roosevelt was too "radical," Miller felt; Hoover represented order. And Miller believed in order. The political judgment of the youthful Miller hardly matters, but the impulse it reflects is telling. Miller is a man who desires and requires an ordered, a coherent world.

Miller is a moralist. A moralist is a man who believes he possesses the truth and aims to convince others of it. In Miller this moralistic trait stems from a strong family feeling. In this context the father as prime authority and guide is central. From *The Man Who Had All the Luck* through *Death of a Salesman* the father stands for virtue and value; to his sons he is the personification of Right and Truth. In *All My Sons* Chris cries out against his father's (Joe Keller's) delinquency. "I know you're no worse than other men but I thought you were better. I never saw you as a man; I saw you as my father." Joe Keller expresses Miller's idealization of the father-son relationship when he exclaims, "I'm his father and he's my son. Nothing's bigger than that."

The shock which shatters Miller's dramatic cosmos always begins with the father's inability to enact the role of moral authority the son assigns to him and which the father willy-nilly assumes. The son never altogether absolves the father for his defection nor is the father ever able to forgive himself for it. Each bears a heavy burden of responsibility to the other. Both may be innocent, but both suffer guilt.

The mother, beloved of father and son, supports the paternal legend of "kingship." She is fealty itself. She is unalterably loyal to the family and the ideal of its necessary cohesion as the basis for the good life, a moral world. The mother's devotion to this ideal constitutes a force which is passive in appearance only. Her influence may be constricting, even injurious, though it is never faulted in Miller's plays. Mrs. Keller in *All My Sons* is indirectly the source of much trouble—she preserves the superstitions of the family and of a blemished society—but while Chris rails at his father he barely challenges his mother. Woman in Miller's plays is usually the prop of the male principle without whom man falters, loses his way.

There is something more personal than such general considerations in Miller's view of the family as the "symbolic" cell of the social structure, the dissolution of which is a threat to life itself. It is simply and passionately articulated in *After the Fall* when its central character, Quentin, blurts out, "I can't bear to be a separate person."

Separateness from our fellow men is a human *non sequitur*.

What in Miller's experience and thought seems the chief cause for the family's crack-up? Where does social fission originate? The Depression of the Thirties was the crucial factor of Miller's formative years; it not only brought hardship to his parents and consequently to their children but it made him realize something else as well. It was not financial stress alone that shook the foundations of American life at that time but a false ideal which the preceding era, the Twenties, had raised to the level of a religious creed: the ideal of Success. The unsuccessful man, the one who failed in business, was a flawed man. Such failure was considered something more than a misfortune; it was the sign of a moral defect. It was turpitude.

Miller has often said that as a college student he was very much affected by a performance of Odets' *Awake and Sing!* he saw in Chicago. That play contained a line which struck the keynote of the period: "Go out and fight so life shouldn't be printed on dollar bills," followed by the even more homely precept: "Life should have some dignity."

In *All My Sons* a small town doctor, disappointed in the inspirational meagreness of his practice murmurs, "Money, money, money, money, money. You say it long enough it doesn't mean anything. How I'd love to be around when that happens!" (Mrs. Keller responds with, "You're so childish, Jim.") In *Death of a Salesman,* Charley, Loman's neighbor, says apropos of Loman, "No man needs only a little salary." And when outraged at Loman's muddle-headedness and feeble sense of reality, his son's basic accusation is that Loman has blown him "full of hot air." It is the hot air of the corrupted American dream, the dream of Success—affluence and status as the ultimate goals of human endeavor.

Willy Loman's worth lies in his natural bent for manual work: he is a craftsman. If he had cultivated that side of himself he might have retained his dignity. But Willy has been seduced by the bitch goddess, Success, by Salesmanship. So he lives in a vacuum, a vapor of meaningless commercial slogans. The irony of Willy's death—his suicide is a distortion of the responsibility he feels toward his son—is embodied in the conviction that only by leaving Biff his insurance money can he fulfill his paternal duty! Willy's hollow "religion" has crippled his faculties, corroded his moral fibre.

Sweet, dumb, nobly ignoble Willy never learns anything. But Miller, and the men of his generation, had begun to. Miller became a "radical." The root of evil was the false ideal. The heart of Miller's radicalism is conservative: it seeks the maintenance of individual dignity within the context of the family which broadens to the concept of society as a whole.

The son becomes the father. He desires to take over authority. The radical becomes the leader, the prophet. Armed with a new insight, arrived at through the father's fall, the son now carries the banner of righteousness and justice. He is no longer simply moral; he is a moraliser, a preacher. Thus he may fall from grace into the pit of self-righteousness.

In *All My Sons* Chris says, "Every man follows a star. The star of his honesty. Once it is out it never lights again." It burns so intensely that Chris virtually wills his father's punishment for having knowingly sent out defective airplane motors to the Army.

The severity of such righteousness often boomerangs. The reforms of the Thirties and early Forties were followed by the repressions of the Fifties. Miller spoke out courageously against the forces of repression. *The Crucible,* written between 1952 and 1953, is still a virile protest against the aberrations of McCarthyism. That the witch-hunt of Salem cannot be equated with the fear of Communism is not valid as a criticism of the play. What *The Crucible* does is to show us a community terrorized into a savagely hysterical fury that is reprehensible whether it is based on fact or on falsehood. The play asks, "Is the accuser always holy now?", a question altogether suitable to the situation of the Fifties. "Vengeance is walking Salem" had become almost literally exact.

The hindsight afforded by *After the Fall* renders perceptible certain secondary aspects of *The Crucible* which passed unnoticed at the time of its production in 1953. Neither John Proctor nor his wife Elizabeth is guilty of witchcraft! Both act in the upright manner we expect of them. (Miller, found guilty of Contempt of Congress in 1956 for refusing to mention the names of people he recognized at a Communist meeting he had attended some years before, was cleared of the charge by the United States Court of Appeals in 1958.) But other guilts are confessed by the Proctors, man and wife, in *The Crucible.* Elizabeth has been guilty of coldness to her husband; John of "lechery." He has been unfaithful. Both suspect that part of their misfortune, the accusation of conspiring with the Devil, and their inability to clear themselves are somehow due to their private failings.

One of the most unmistakable features of Miller's work, as we have noted, is what might be called its moralism, or if you will, its Puritanism. There is a traditional sort of tenderness, even a trace of sentimentality, in the early Miller plays. The woman is sweetly yearned for and serves as mate and mainstay to keep her man confident. There is little or no hint of any sensual appreciation of women. In *Death of a Salesman*

Biff feels nothing but horror at Willy's pathetic fling on the road. Desire plays little part in the configuration of dramatic elements in any of Miller's plays before *The Crucible* and enters the scene obliquely and, as it were, shamefacedly as a prop to the plot in *A View from the Bridge*.

The Puritan conscience is a complex phenomenon. Even while it holds fast to its conviction of rightness, it is haunted by a need for the expiation of its own sins. There is nothing for which it feels itself entirely blameless. Man must pay and pay and pay—for everything. The ever-fortunate youth in *The Man Who Had All the Luck* does not consider himself safe until he suffers a most damaging defeat. His partial but painful setback is a warrant to him that he may go forward in his life with some degree of assurance that no greater disaster will befall him. What the Puritan hankers for is total innocence, and it torments him to understand that it cannot possibly be achieved.

Even the pursuit of righteousness and truth seems to the thorough-going Puritan a virtuous aggressiveness which is itself not wholly innocent. It may mask a drive for power. Thus Biff in *Salesman*, as later Quentin in *After the Fall*, questions his own good faith. Sue Bayliss, the down-to-earth doctor's wife in *All My Sons*, wants Chris, avenging angel or conscience of the play, to move away from the neighborhood. "Chris," she says, "makes people want to be better than it is possible to be . . . I resent being next door to the Holy Family. It makes me feel like a bum." The sentiment is psychologically and sociologically sound—reformers disturb public quiet—but what is especially to be remarked here is that in all his plays Miller gives evidence of wanting to move away from himself in this regard. It worries him that he sits in judgment, that he is placing himself in a position to which he has no right. It is as if Miller felt himself a Reverend Davidson who anticipates and desires his own humbling.

To speak of this aspect of Miller's artistic physiognomy as a flaw would be to miss the tension which gives Miller's work its peculiar fascination. The wish to expiate sins of pride, bad faith or moral arrogance are related to a sense of responsibility which lends stature to Miller's work and makes it intimately moving. We are not, we must not be, separate one from the other. Our refusal to acknowledge this and to act upon it is the sin which secretly torments us and causes us profound grief.

Miller harbors an abiding affection for his least striking play, *A Memory of Two Mondays*. This is understandable because in this play he seems at rest, relaxed from the strictures of his central theme. In this play he recalls without blame or debate the simple, undemanding, unself-consciously oppressed folk with whom he worked at the Tenth Avenue warehouse before he entered the world of assertion and moral combat. Here he dwelled without the exposing glare of critical self-examination. The warehouse, gehenna of purposeless toil, was his paradise; like infancy, it was free from the burden of ethical choice.

The repose of this short play is followed immediately by the travail of *A View from the Bridge,* the last of Miller's plays before the "silent" years. In a sense this play is an adjunct to *The Crucible.* While the blemish on Proctor's purity is a contributing factor to his calvary, the personal motivation in *A View from the Bridge* obscures its theme almost as much as it reveals it. For this play dramatizes the passion of betrayal. A decent man is led to squealing on his kin because of jealousy.

Eddie Carbone does not recognize his motivation; this would mortify him. He must rationalize his act on moral grounds. So much is made of Carbone's adulterous and semi-incestuous drive towards his niece that we are apt to miss the fact that what is at stake is not the psychology of sexual turmoil but of duplicity, the man's inability to live up to the obligations of comradeship. We must not force others to pay for the agony of our own weakness.

Miller is compassionate with Carbone; yet he is angry with him. He is compassionate because he feels in himself the bewilderment involved in the sexual impulse, particularly when repressed; he is angry because Carbone is a liar as all men are who conceal their confusion or corruption in an honorable cloak. Miller not only implies that Carbone craves punishment for his delation, he also believes Carbone deserves death. Still Miller, as a humane Puritan, shrinks from so full a measure of condemnation—"an eye for an eye"—and he has his "chorus," in the person of Alfieri, the lawyer-narrator, say, "Most of the time now we settle for half. And I like it better." One suspects that Alfieri says this with a certain trembling as if he were not certain that he does "like it better," that Alfieri feels that the terrible justice which slays Carbone or has him slay himself is the nobler.

We must resume a listing of further biographical data. Miller was married to Mary Slattery, a fellow student at the University of Michigan, in 1942. She bore him two children: a girl now [1968] nineteen and a boy sixteen. He divorced Mary Miller in 1956. He then married Marilyn Monroe. He wrote *The Misfits* for her, a film about the lone worker in a society of industrial mass production. It is a film, he admits, marred by too many cross-purposes. (*The Misfits* was the only one of Miller's film scripts to go before the cameras. Another, called *The Hook,* written with Elia Kazan's encouragement, dealt with racketeering on the waterfront and was about to be produced by Columbia Pictures. The production was abandoned when pressure from certain unions in the film industry was brought to bear on the picture company.) After his divorce from Marilyn Monroe, Miller married Inge Morath, an Austrian-born photographer, in 1961. A daughter, Rebecca, was born to them in 1962.

Two features of *After the Fall* are immediately noticeable. It is the first of Miller's plays where the main emphasis is almost entirely personal. It is also the first Miller play where the largest part of the action concerns itself with marital relationships.

Still *After the Fall* is not only an extension of the themes to be found in Miller's previous plays; it is a reaffirmation through a reversal. The strenuous moralist, the man whose family—the mother in particular—dedicated him to great accomplishments, has come to the middle point of his life and brings himself to trial. He not only confesses, he accuses himself. The jury is his *alter ego*—in the audience; the evidence is provided by the testimony of his memory. His self-assurance has gone. As many in our time, he is "hung up"; he despairs.

He now finds the continuous "litigation of existence" pointless because the judge's seat is empty. There is no "father," no supreme arbiter. He will have to allow us, the audience, to judge him. Why is the trial held? Not so that he may be condemned or that the charges brought be dismissed but so that he regain his capacity to "move on." He is seeking the hope which lies beyond despair, the life which renews itself after the fall, with the death of the old self. He wants to bury himself as an Idea and find himself as a Person.

The lawyer, Quentin, who was sent forth in his youth with a Mission to fulfill a destiny in the light of some "star," now begins to recollect the specific circumstances of his past—people and events—instead of patterning them on a principle. "To see endangers principle," he says. The examination of conscience through a review of the precise detail in the crisis of his life exposes his self-delusions, hypocrisies, insufficiencies, falterings and confusions. He is now skeptical of abstracts, even the abstract of Despair.

The tangle of lives in the play's broad canvas, the complexity and contradiction of motives in his former search for a moral victory lead him to an understanding of his, and possibly our universal, complicity in wrongdoing. We who denounce the hangman are ourselves executioners. We assume powers we do not possess. We undertake tasks it is not within our means to complete. The proposition that we are not separate takes on a new meaning; a new light is shed on the injunction of human responsibility. Each of us is separate and in our separateness we must assume responsibility even in full awareness of that separateness.

Thus Quentin may survive after the fall through a recognition of his own place among the accused, a realization of his role as an accomplice in the misdeeds he has denounced. The judge's bench is not on high; it is in the common court of our lives together. We are all both the jailers and prisoners of the concentration camps. The acceptance of the defeat in this realization may liberate the man dogged by having had "all the luck"—and answers! There are no guarantees for any choice we make, but one is never absolved from the necessity of making choices and of paying for them.

The struggle represented in all of Miller's work, of which *After the Fall* is a central turning point, achieves a special eloquence for us in the American particularity of its tone and speech. There is a plainness, a kind of neighborhood friendliness and good humor, one might say a saving ordinariness, which gives Miller's dialogue a special appeal. The literary or aesthetic "purist" who deplores this element of Miller's talent is as remote from our reality as those who once found nothing more in Huckleberry Finn than a story for kids.

Miller is a popular writer. This may be a limitation but it is more probably a strength. Those who wept over Willy Loman, whether his story exemplifies true Tragedy or not, are closer to the truth of our day than those who want it told to them in monumental or quasi-mythical symbols for all time.

There is besides the comforting familiarity of Miller's expression an enthusiasm which mingles a deep-rooted American idealism with an age-old Hebraic fervor, a quality which mounts from hearth and home to the elevation of an altar. Miller's dialogue, coined from the energetic and flavorsome palaver of the streets, is finally wrought into something close to prophetic incantation.

After the Fall is a signal step in the evolution of Arthur Miller as man and artist. The play's auto-criticism exposes him to us; it also liberates him so that he can go on free of false legend and heavy halo. Had he not written this play he might never have been able to write another. We may now look to a future of ever more creative effort.

II. Director's Notes: *Incident at Vichy*

Explanation

My notes precede the making of the "director's book" in which, on a separate sheet beside almost every line, I set down the action, the adjustment, the physical movement or business (if any) of each scene. This might be called the "score" of the stage play. It is from this that the actors are directed. [A sample of the director's book for *Incident at Vichy* is on pages 162–63.]

The notes which follow are intended for myself alone—to direct me! They indicate what I feel and think about the approach to the play and its characters. Strictly speaking, there is no need for a director to make such notes or at least to put them in writing. But I find that unless I write them down I am not sure I have thought precisely enough and will be able to make my ideas sufficiently clear and cogent for the actors. I do not, however, read these notes to them. Their essence must be conveyed to the cast more freely, less "intellectually," by gesture, demonstration, anecdote, dramatic example, trial and error on the stage.

At first the notes are set down haphazardly in no particular order, without too definite a method. After five or six readings of the script— more in the case of a very complex play—I read through each of the individual character's lines, setting down the basic action or motivation, the attitudes, peculiar traits or history of each of them. Only then do I begin to work on the main body of my *preparatory* work, which is the director's book. The operative work is done at rehearsals.

In the director's book for *Incident at Vichy* the first notation reads: "General action: to wait, to know—in motionless anxiety. . . . In the half-light the characters on the bench are seen in 'frozen' psychologic postures—as if they were statues. Hold for thirty seconds." This idea was more or less abandoned by me because the effect did not come off, due to the special (and also inadequate) repertory lighting arrangement at the ANTA Washington Square Theatre. What I intended could only be telling if the unrealistic, altogether stylized nature of this "business" could be immediately recognized as such by the audience. There is still a remnant of this notion in a more naturalistic vein in the present production.

" 'Cautious' atmosphere of mutual distrust," my first direction reads. "Lights come up. Another thirty-second pause. [The painter] Lebeau observes the others on bench and speaks his first line—'Cup of coffee would be nice. Even a sip'—to arouse attention, to make contact with others . . .'"

The Notes

AN IMPRESSION ON MY FIRST READING OF THE SCRIPT (JULY 11TH, '64)

The Play: A medallion or emblem engraved on metal or stone. When the curtain rises [there is no curtain at the ANTA Washington Square Theatre] two pauses: one in which the characters remain immobile—arrayed as if in a "memorial tablet" or "frieze" in commemoration of the dead. Then they move as living characters—slowly. There is a long wait of anxiety. They are in a hell of expectancy, uneasiness, bewilderment, wonder.

Business? The Prince gives the Boy's ring to Leduc. [This business and an accompanying line was not in the original script. I suggested it to Miller who added the line and business at rehearsal.]

The Old Jew is a "chorus"—his behavior is a spiritual pantomime. He's praying . . . he's waiting, he despairs, he pleads for mercy (of God). His gestures and attitudes are an unconscious running commentary on what is being said.

The others (in their silence) must run the gamut of indifference, self-absorption, fear, horror, a desire to interrupt, to object, to stop the conversation, to watch what is going on in the office behind them, etc.

AUGUST 12TH. Conversation with Boris Aronson about the setting. It must seem constructed of metal and stone. Its locale not too specific. [Originally it was called "a police station." Changed by Miller to "a place of detention."] The fact that the play presumably takes place in Vichy not important. A first sketch rejected as rather too decorative—though macabre. Something hard, mysterious, "Kafka-like" desired. A "no-man's land" enclosure.

CASTING. Bob Whitehead suggests Joseph Wiseman as the Actor, David Stewart as the (Communist) Worker. I prefer Wiseman as Leduc the Psychoanalyst, Stewart as the Actor. An actor outside the Permanent Company suggested for the Prince. I prefer David Wayne. All my casting unanimously accepted by Whitehead, Kazan, Miller.

EARLY NOTES (BEFORE SETTING DOWN CHARACTER DESCRIPTION)

The Prince [Von Berg] is distracted, hesitant, uncertain as if slightly "gaga." He is puzzled. Diffident. Then deeply troubled.

The characters have been detained. Confined. "Imprisoned." Why? They do not know. They question: why? why? why? The first action is to learn, discover the reason. They are worried and confused, and they "hope"—a concomitant of anxiety.

How explain their detention?

Because they are Jews? Is the Business Man a Jew? Is the Gypsy a Jew? Is the Prince a Jew?

And if they are Jews, does that mean they must die? Why?

What can save them?

Believing in the Working Class Revolution? Belief in Art? Belief in God?

Or must they fight?

All this resolves itself to "What's to be done?" Is there no hope? What? What? What?

The answer is to take responsibility. The "revolt" of responsibility without any guarantee except the belief that each must help the other.

This suggests that the "spine" of the play has to do with the anguished (bewildered) quest: an attempt to discover the answer to the question, the meaning of and "remedy" for *evil*—which consists, [the Doctor] Leduc says, in "the fear and hatred of the 'other.' "

Apropos of this Leduc asks, "Is there a reasonable explanation of your sitting here? But you are sitting here, aren't you?"

The Actor exclaims, "But an atrocity like that (burning Jews) is beyond belief." To which the reply is, "That is exactly the point."

All (except the Gestapo "Professor," the Police) *ask questions.* The Police and the Gestapo have the answers—through their superiors. Even the self-torturing Major asks a question: why is he allowing himself to do what he is doing? He asks, "Why do you deserve to live more than I do?"

How many ways are there to "act" tension, anguish?

Begin rehearsals quickly, with simple and clear actions, not fully expressed. Do not attempt "big emotions" at first.

They stand up when it is impossible to remain seated.

"Does anybody know *any*thing?" This is the key to the spine and mood of the play. (The play might be called *The Waiting Room*.) They are waiting for an answer to a question to which there is no "answer."

THE SPINE OF THE PLAY:

To find the answer (to the "trap" = evil), the way out of the dilemma in which they are imprisoned.

THE SPINE OF CHARACTERS AND THEIR "CHARACTERISTICS":

VON BERG (THE PRINCE)

Spine: To learn (*see*) the situation fully for the first time.

He doesn't know the answer. He doesn't even know the question. He's vague, confused. he has lived apart from the central reality.

Life has passed him by; he's out of the mainstream. Hence his diffidence, sense of frustration which brings him close to tears. Very gentle and polite.

"Bewildered." His first question is a clue: "Excuse me. Have you all been arrested for being Jewish?" And his second remark: "I'm terribly sorry. *I had no idea.*" Very shaken by the discovery.

Long silences of "confusion." He's trying to puzzle it all out . . . he's intuitive (romantic) rather than intellectual. Almost "sweet," naïve. ("I am Viennese.")

He's modest: the nobleman is a forgotten man, a relic. "Vulgarity" is the supreme sin. It bespeaks coarseness, lack of feeling.

He considers things very carefully, speaks diffidently unless intuitively certain. He's always apologizing.

His final action is explained only by the fact that he is a man of feeling, not of calculation. His is the pure impetus of the truly moved person, the basic impulse of love. Even in the Major's office he is not yet aware of what he will do a minute later.

He wants to believe the best = he hopes for amelioration. That is why it takes him so long to realize the worst.

He asks the cardinal question of the play and of our time: "But what is left if one gives up one's ideals?"

He grieves for the world . . . his final gesture is not intended by him to *prove* anything: it is a spontaneous burst of his innermost self.

Psychologic gestures:

(a) A timid and pained movement of hand to inquire or learn.

(b) Lowering of head in pain or shame.

(c) A suddenly fierce resolve and affirmation.

LEDUC

Spine: To see it through to the end . . . intellectually and physically.

His is an *active* mind. It seeks to find answers which work. It is a "fighting" mind. It is a firm, unhysterical mind, courageous, with the will to accomplish an end.

Reason is a weapon to be handled with care, caution, and respect. It can liberate. There is the thrust of a blade in this man's spirit but it is controlled by his humanism. He has passion but it is not indiscriminate; it is held in check by his professional training and the discipline which that entails.

Hence he is willing to fight, to kill if that is the only way out. He tries to understand, to plan. Remember: he was a soldier, an officer.

He is inclined to "pessimism," through a scientific or objective recognition of the facts. But—less consciously—he desires a "mitigation" of the facts. He is more moralist than he realizes. (Perhaps this is his "Jewishness.") Though reason (rationalism) prevents him from hoping excessively. He is "appalled" by Von Berg's action, though he has admitted to the Major that he would be ready to escape alone.

"Come on, we can do something" is fundamental to his character.

"I am being as impersonal as I know how to be." It is not easy but the impulse *to understand* is constantly present.

His "scientific" assurances place him against a blank wall which even he cannot bear or altogether accept. Hence his tension, his ultimate bafflement. He is less "released" than Von Berg. (Von Berg's inexplicable, unreasoned action is more meaningful and more valuable finally than Leduc's knowledge and confirmed data. Leduc may learn something his reason could not reveal to him.)

When Leduc tells Von Berg that man is full of hate of the other, this "dreadful truth" is a form of self-crucifixion . . . a desire to put some terrible blame on himself.

Psychologic gesture: Control. The desire to point out . . . with a thrusting finger of examination and diagnosis. Then grasping his head to lessen the agony of his own contradictory pulls.

LEBEAU (THE PAINTER)

Spine: To ask the question.

With all this bespeaks of fear, anxiety, hope, confusion, and final fatigue.

An innocent. He feels "guilty" somehow—because he is innocent. (His "escape"—coffee!)

The average man of sensibility. Knows he can't understand—but thoroughly honest about it. (The artist!) He is certainly frightened because he has no answer: in this respect he is the most "normal" person of the lot. ("You wouldn't have any idea what's going on, would you?") He's hungry, nervous, he wishes he were somewhere else, he is almost ready to die of tiredness. It's all torment, but not "pessimism." He's simply a feeling person of our time.

The surprise, the indignity, the madness of having his nose measured!

He's in sympathy with almost everybody who is "nice." Observe how he speaks to the Gypsy.

Likes to talk, to "philosophize." He is the artist without many fixed ideas, only feelings and the heritage of a liberal culture.

"What kind of crew is this? The animosity!" This is the natural man (or artist) who resents or is offended by "closed" people—the Business Man *et al.*

Alternates between trembling fear and sweet hope . . . "nervous" hope.

"Good papers." Oh, the little things that can give one courage, a sense of stability. *Repetition* of self-assurance.

No realist he. He can only paint what he imagines. He has a need to be with others, to feel himself with others, but the others being more "practical" hold back.

Psychologic gesture: arms apart, questioning the world. Then dropping them in discouragement.

BAYARD (THE WORKER—ELECTRICIAN)

Spine: To stand by and save himself by his answer or social conviction.

His conviction—the triumph of socialism—keeps him erect, sustains, fortifies him. (His costume, typical of the French worker, should have some of the "stiffness" of armor!) He has earned his answer by a life of work and struggle.

He's watchful, alert, ever "on the ready." He's learned how to take care of himself, fight if need be.

He's helpful: to Lebeau for example. Wishes to cooperate, work with others. He's not impulsive; he's strong, contained. Somewhat "didactic" in the leftist manner. Not entirely without humor. But downright!

(Use of French popular gestures.)

There is vigor (quiet or explosive) in all his utterances.

Psychologic gesture: shoulders set, jaw tight, clenched upright fist.

MONCEAU (THE ACTOR)

Spine: To live by the ideal of his cultural environment, his "public." He's a bourgeois idealist: as an artist I serve the public, my country, humanity. This is my justification and my support.

A certain dignified hauteur. A certain *histrionic* "simplicity." A conscious pose of modesty.

Still there is *le geste, panache,* the courage and pride of the stage. Dresses conservatively off-stage with only a hint of the theatrically self-conscious. There is here the mixture of the academic (French Establishment) and the discreetly Bohemian. He's tense withal.

It is the bourgeois in him which assumes the "sensible" attitude in everything. But like so many actors of this kind, he is not altogether secure, though usually in an optimistic frame of mind. He vacillates and may at times be superstitious . . . Still he clings to his ideal to the end . . .

He has eloquence, a forensic ability both French and theatrical.

Psychologic gesture: He stands at attention with a tendency to throw his head backward employing graceful gestures (*noblesse*).

THE MAJOR

Spine: To carry out orders.

But he has been wounded and he is no longer sure of his ability or desire to carry out orders. But what else is there for him to do?

So he is "caught" too . . . sickened by the compulsion to follow orders. Still he tries not to listen to the voices of his doubt or guilt. He fights them off as symptoms of weakness. He almost hates himself for suffering from these symptoms and hates those who provoke them in him. He would like to prove that he has no cause to harbor any doubt.

He hates to talk to the Prisoners, tries to avoid them. Tries, because of his ambivalence, to "appease" Leduc and, failing that, to subdue him as the embodiment of his guilt. For a man with his job he suffers the fatal weakness of feeling!

He's at the breaking point. He wants to calm himself with drink which only stimulates the pain of his various wounds. When he fires the gun, it is a signal to himself and the others: *Schluss!* Shut up, you Jews; shut up, my soul! Get on with the job: we're all under orders anyway.

Like many Germans, he is a semi-disciplined or controlled hysteric.

He's "tempted" to break ranks, to defy the Professor. This is the specific and immediate cause of his tension. The debate with himself is carried on through his confrontations with the Professor, Leduc, even with the Old Jew!

After his scene with Leduc he resumes the procedure of examination, savagely confident that he will now be able to follow the Gestapo orders. He very nearly "glories" in the fact that he shall succeed in doing so.

Psychologic gesture: Stands with clenched teeth, tight fist, trying to carry on with power, determined eye and yet he never is wholly secure.

THE PROFESSOR

Spine: To carry out or perform the answer.

The Enemy ("evil") is anyone or anything standing in the way of the Third Reich. He functions through will, science, and force.

(He dresses very correctly. Like a "polished" university bureaucrat.)

He is *"absolute."* His certainty makes him dangerous, quietly fierce. He's in command.

Psychologic gesture: Cold imperious eyes (he wears glasses). Straight-backed, efficiently spare in gesture and movement.

THE WAITER

Spine: To worm out of trouble.

The most defenseless of all the characters. Timid, always "friendly," obsequious, terrified by his humble position. (He feels superior to the Gypsy only.) He makes friends through *café* and *croissants.*

Perhaps he is an emigré from Poland . . . already terrified there. Now
he hates "irregularity." He finds comfort only in the quiet nest of the
bistro or café where he works. He *leans* on people, looking to the strong
for protection (his native-born French boss, the important customers including the Major). He tries to smile his way out of trouble. Always seeking to be reassured by authority. A "schnook."

He's the only one who tries to flee in terror and is seen to be beaten.
The only one thoroughly cowed. (He's naturally very pale.)

Psychologic gesture: Smiling and crouching away as if ready for flight;
that is, when he's not leaning on someone for protection. Looks as if he
were always prepared for a slap. Compensates by always trying to in-
gratiate himself.

MARCHAND (THE BUSINESS MAN)

Spine: To do important work. To be in the center of activity. (Should
be rather comic in effect.)

He is annoyed, indignant at his being detained. He's carrying on the
business of the world, of France in the moment of its need.

He puts people "down" because he is right. Condescension is natural
to him. He knows the answers.

Obsequious in a "reputable" manner to authority. He's "above" the
situation. He sounds as if he were giving orders reasonably yet with a
touch of indignation.

(The French bourgeois knows how to fix and correct everything. He
always complains about the government and the powers that be.)

Psychologic gesture: Impatience. Sits on edge of chair. A kind of pushing in his desire to get on. He throws his weight around. Waddles with
impatience, walks rapidly.

POLICE CAPTAIN

Spine: To get even.

Vengeful because of hurts—real and imagined—suffered all his life.
People have been getting away with murder: now men of my sort have a
chance to get rid of all the vermin—wipe them out.

The knowing smile of a mean twirp. Squints, grins with malice and
"shrewdness." He is at once "sneaky" and obsequious in regard to the
Germans.

Cutting voice.

Psychologic gesture: A malicious smirk on his face like a man about to play a dirty trick or discover something which will justify his pleasure in punishment. Walks with noiseless tread.

GYPSY

Spine: To disregard it all.

He's used to being arrested. He's a vagrant. Indifferent. He's waiting for What? He's disconnected from the others, from their problems.

He's sure he'll get out of the jam somehow . . . hardly concerned. The others are all "strangers," "outsiders." They are hostile forces of nature to be avoided, not to be fought with. One must deal with them as best one can.

He doesn't laugh; he grins. Not a grin of amusement but rather a protective coloring. It may look idiotic or sinister. A mechanical response. "If it were possible I'd like to cut your guts out"—is his secret thought.

His voice whines a bit on "No steal." "Fix." The "whine" is not an expression of sorrow but rather a plea or an assurance made for the thousandth time.

Psychologic gesture: He abstracts himself from his environment, generally turned away from the others.

BOY

Spine: To take care of his mother.

The son of Polish Jewish parents. He's been in trouble most of his life. Worked hard, concerned only with protecting his mother. (Father died in 1932.)

Intelligent, aware, sensitive. Quietly trying to survive. Taut, attentive and spunky. His main idea: "How can I get the money to my mother if I fail to get out?" His courage is an extension of the love for his mother. That is why he attempts to "jail break."

Psychologic gesture: He's bent over in the pose of "The Thinker," turned toward the corridor door—*the way out.* (The Gypsy is turned away in the opposite direction: he has no intention of escaping. The Boy is straining toward the only point of egress.)

The **Major** *enters the corridor at its far end. The* **Boy** *halts,* **Leduc**
*beside him. For a moment they stand facing him. Then they turn and
come down the corridor and sit, the* **Major** *following them. He touches*
Leduc's *sleeve, and* **Leduc** *stands and follows him downstage.*

Major, *he is "high"—with drink and a flow of emotion.* That's impossible. Don't try it. There are sentries on both corners. *Glancing
toward the office door.* I would only like to say that . . . this is all
as inconceivable to me as it is to you. Can you believe that?

Leduc. I'd believe it if you shot yourself. And better yet, if you took a
few of them with you.

Major, *wiping his mouth with the back of his hand.* We would all be
replaced by tomorrow morning, wouldn't we.

Leduc. We might get out alive, though; you could see to that.

Major. They'd find you soon.

Leduc. Not me.

Major, *with a manic amusement, yet deeply questioning.* Why do you
deserve to live more than I do?

Leduc. Because I am incapable of doing what you are doing. I am better
for the world than you.

Major. It means nothing to you that I have feelings about this?

Leduc. Nothing whatever, unless you get us out of here.

Major. And then what? Then what?

Leduc. I will remember a decent German, an honorable German.

Major. Will that make a difference?

Leduc. I will love you as long as I live. Will anyone do that now?

Major. That means so much to you?—that someone love you?

Leduc. That I be worthy of someone's love, yes. And respect.

Major. It's amazing; you don't understand anything. Nothing of that
kind is left, don't you understand that yet?

Leduc. It is left in me.

Major, *more loudly.* There are no persons any more, don't you see that?
There will never be persons again. What do I care if you love me?
Are you out of your mind? What am I, a dog that I must be loved?
You . . . *turning to all of them* . . . goddamned Jews!

This page from Harold Clurman's "Director's Book" for *Incident at Vichy* is keyed
line-by-line to the text page printed opposite it.

		Confrontation for a second
To "make friends" To take advantage of a soft spot	Sotto voce: not too warm	
	"Tempted".. but honest and to the point	
	Shrewd . . . a little sour-sweet	*The Deep Debate* and Difference Intense and quiet
	Quietly hard	
	Between bitterness and hate	N O T T O O F A S T
	Getting riled—a slow boil of agony	
	Exasperated—on the verge of hysteria	
	Screams in pain!	

The above dialogue from *Incident at Vichy* is on pp. 53–54 of the published text (New York: Viking Press, 1965).

FERRAND (THE CAFÉ BOSS)

Spine: To get along.

In an incomprehensible world which he has long since given up questioning or understanding. He is all "adjustment."

Trying to please the customers, the powers that be, always scurrying and in a sweat.

Weeps with fright, with sorrow, with impotence: inability to help, fear of becoming "involved."

Psychologic gesture: the hurry and bustle of service.

DETECTIVES

Spine: To ape the Captain.

Without an opinion. They have no business with an opinion. They are the "mutes" of the world, those who stand by and do not interfere with superior force.

THE OLD JEW

Spine: To endure *in faith.*

He has been in hiding. He is dragged onto stage. He is neither hero nor victim. He has become "resigned" since he has no weapon against evil except faith, which is something between himself and the Almighty. He does not fret over trouble. He is inured to pain to the point of death. He is above fear, he will not break under torture. For him, endurance itself is meaningful. He is aware of the "atmosphere" around him. He prays . . . he remembers, he sighs in sorrow, he pleads (with God) that he may come to understand, he falls in a faint. He "resists" in his spirit.

He is not the "abject" Jew though he may be the "external wanderer" or the eternally pursued. Sorrowful or exalted he may be but not "little," martyred but never degraded. His eye accuses his tormentor.

III. The Merits of Mr. Miller

In Bernard Shaw's comedy "You Never Can Tell," a well-educated man, when asked if he thinks a proposed marriage is unwise, replies,

"Yes, I do: All matches are unwise. It's unwise to be born; it's unwise to be married; and it's unwise to live, and it's wise to die." To which the gentleman's unlettered father interjects, "So much the worse for wisdom."

In Arthur Miller's "Incident at Vichy" an Austrian nobleman, Von Berg, offers to sacrifice his life for the Jewish doctor who will certainly be sent to a concentration camp and probably to his death by the Nazis. Von Berg is an esthete: he despises the Nazis in the first place because they are "vulgar." He possesses almost no political insight. When he comes on the scene he is hesitant, embarrassed and on the whole rather unaware of the depths of Nazi depravity. His sudden impulse to self-sacrifice is "unwise."

Von Berg, unlike Chris in "All My Sons," never preaches. He acts through a rush of feeling which he doesn't question. What he does is not at all "sensible" but we understand its reason.

Shaw, more gifted in ratiocination and argument than Miller, employed reason to justify the irrational—something he associated with Henri Bergson's *élan vital* or life force. Miller, with less philosophy, is similarly motivated. His people often behave like fools but are driven by emotions or instincts they do not comprehend. We however understand them.

By temperament Miller is a moralist, even a Puritan. In a somewhat different context I once wrote, "The puritan conscience is a complex phenomenon. . . . Even the pursuit of righteousness and truth to a thoroughgoing puritan seems an aggressiveness [of pride] which is itself not wholly innocent. . . . In all his plays Miller gives evidence of wanting to move away from himself in this regard. It worries him that he sits in judgment, that he is placing himself in a position to which he believes he has no right. It is as if Miller felt himself a Reverend Davidson who anticipates and desires his own 'humbling.' "

I now retract one statement in this passage. Only Miller's later plays reveal this trait of self-doubt. In one instance it becomes self-castigation. This turn in Miller's work alters the form of his plays since "All My Sons." That play and the one which preceded it are conventional realism. "Death of a Salesman" and "After the Fall" tend to reach beyond a narrow naturalism, while "Incident at Vichy" and "The Price" follow the classic model—unity of time and place—and in their continuity and density of action take on qualities of parable.

A close look at Miller's text may cast a new interpretive light on his work. Willy Loman is certainly no "hero." He is surely no "man who seeks or finds the right way to live." In having Loman's younger son Happy say at his father's funeral, "Willy Loman did not die in vain. He had a good dream," Miller is clearly adding an ironic character touch. If the circumstances were different, it would be comic. For Happy has learned nothing from the family tragedy just as Willy's suicide is the climax of his own absurdity. The dream which ruined Willy was to be a success in all the ways which were alien to his nature. Willy's merit is that he was an honest craftsman—he was good at making things—but he bought the latter-day American dream which is to make oneself "well liked" by storing up a pile, riding an expensive car, having one's name in the papers, etc. etc. Loman has displaced his *self* in an almost universally prevalent falsity. He commits suicide so that his son Biff may have a chance to make good, in other words, to succeed in pursuing the same misguided path which has blighted his own and his family's existence. Happy, in contrast to his father, plans to "make it." The "ideal" for which Willy lived and dies, Miller shows us, is a disastrous one, consequently not at all one he asks us to admire.

Carbone in "A View from the Bridge" cannot conceivably be regarded as a "hero." The play is a study in shameful rationalization. A jealous man betrays another and justifies himself on specious grounds: patriotism, horror at homosexuality. Miller's puritan streak—though it is something more than that—consists of having Carbone finally desire his own death: he cannot live with his own lie.

There is a parallel in "The Crucible." It is chiefly a study in mass hysteria in which superstition conspires with self-interest to incite a society to destructiveness. Proctor accepts death not only as an act of moral defiance but also because he suspects himself of guilt: "lechery."

The change which I detect in Miller (and on the whole it marks a progress) is caused by the tension of an uncertainty in him. I have never believed that Miller proposed to exonerate Quentin in "After the Fall," or in any way succeeded in doing so. Quentin in that play has always struck me as less honest and likable than either of his two wives. The play is a moralist's accusation of self-deception and duplicity. Quentin has pretended—with little more than maternal encouragement and a "good head"—to act like a scion of the "holy family." He discovers his fallibility and since the "judge's seat" is empty (there is for him no God to whom he can appeal) he vows, despite the whole world's callousness and brutality, to point no self-righteous finger at others; he must himself first find the way back to a truth which his innermost being can substantiate in action. That is *his* morality. It is also new for Miller. The moralist in him now dictates "Put up or shut up."

Does Victor Franz in "The Price" unequivocally assume the stature of a hero or a victor? His behavior is hardly "reasonable." He has given up an opportunity for a good career to aid a father he knew or suspected was by no means an exemplary figure. He clings to a deeply rooted feeling that he was bound to act as he did though it may have been "unwise." Miller's sympathy is clearly with Victor but if he "sides" with him it is not without painful doubt. That is why some folk leave the theater with the conviction that Walter, the "selfish" brother, is in the right and Victor indeed a failure.

The play is so written, the ending so understated that its "lesson" is to some extent left undetermined. The audience takes the furniture man Solomon to its heart: he is the common citizen, the honest man without pretentions. He is the mediator who sees both sides of the question and is therefore endowed with wonderful humor, the kind of humor which endears him to all of us. It is just this trace of ambiguity—foregoing his earlier dogmatism—which is significant of Miller's development.

More vital than this to an appreciation of the play is that, while it may be well liked, it also disturbs. It disturbs because it is not exactly what we want to hear. In so far as Miller "irrationally" insists that we follow the rule of responsibility beyond our own immediate or egotistic interests, whether it be the family, a social group or ideal—and all these may also be our *ideals,* representative, in other words, of our professed beliefs—the effort to do so troubles almost more than it reassures us. Most of us are ready to act with a sense of responsibility only when it is easy or convenient.

We live in a world which by its operative custom persuades us to follow Willy Loman's dream and to assent to Happy's apparently ineradicable will to imitate it. (Goethe said it: "You think you're pushing, but you're shoved.") Deny it though we do, success as the measure of man still shapes our way of life, and only a memory of another, more ancient faith, and our continued pretense that we abide by it, makes us resent facing the fact that we are doing nothing of the kind.

The power of "The Price," and it is powerful despite the triviality of some of its details, is that whether we "stand" with Victor or with Walter an issue crucial to all our lives is unmistakably posed. Those who "agree" with Victor's self-sacrifice are rendered disquiet because they do not actually live as he has; those who are inclined to Walter's practical mode of thinking are troubled by the suggestion that they are being accused and require defense. "The Price" stirs even those in the audience who may not be "pleased" with it. It pierces our vital centers. That is why some weep and others say, as they did about Willy Loman, that they have a cousin, an uncle, a brother-in-law just like Victor or Walter but very rarely "like me."

Miller's resolution, even under the pressure of some of his own misgivings, to hold fast to a traditional morality is against the grain of our times, against much of our contemporary literature and drama which willy-nilly celebrate cynicism, negativism, collapse, or either a lofty or a comfortable unconcern for responsible ideas sustained by action. This resistance to our souls' sloth dramatized through the humble folk of our land and time defines Miller's signal contribution to the American theater of our day. About the stage effectiveness of Miller's plays there is no dispute. Our audiences and those from London to Tokyo testify to it.

To point out that Miller is not the equal of Ibsen is an irrelevance. It is also an evasion of duty to what is real, immediate and needed in our country and in our lives presumably on the basis of an absolute esthetic purity in which none of us who goes to the theater dwells or should dwell. Our heirs will draw up the balance sheet—and even they may not be "right."

Chronology of Important Dates

1915   Arthur Miller born in New York City.

1936   Attends University of Michigan. First play, *Honors at Dawn,* produced. Wins Avery Hopwood Award.

1938   *No Villain* wins Hopwood Award and Theatre Guild Prize. Miller graduates from Michigan and joins the Federal Theatre Project.

1940   Marries Mary Slattery.

1944   *The Man Who Had All The Luck*—his first Broadway production. *Situation Normal* published.

1945   His novel, *Focus,* published.

1947   *All My Sons* produced.

1949   *Death of a Salesman* produced and wins Pulitzer Prize.

1950   His adaptation of Ibsen's *An Enemy of the People* produced.

1953   *The Crucible* produced.

1955   *A Memory of Two Mondays* and the one-act version of *A View from the Bridge* produced.

1956   He appears before House Un-American Activities Committee and refuses to inform on others. The revised two-act version of *A View from the Bridge* produced in London. Receives an honorary doctorate from the University of Michigan. Divorces Mary Slattery and marries Marilyn Monroe.

1957   Convicted for contempt of Congress. *Collected Plays* published.

1958   Contempt conviction reversed. Elected to the National Institute of Arts and Letters.

1960   He and Marilyn Monroe divorced.

1961   *The Misfits* released.

1962   Marries Inge Morath; daughter Rebecca born.

1964   *After The Fall* is premiere production of Repertory Theatre of Lincoln Center. *Incident at Vichy* also produced there.

1965   Elected International President of P.E.N. (Poets, Essayists, and Novelists).

1967   *I Don't Need You Any More,* a collection of short stories, published.

1968   *The Price* produced.

Notes on the Editor and Contributors

ROBERT W. CORRIGAN, the editor of this volume, is President of the California Institute of the Arts. Previously, he was Dean of the School of the Arts of New York University. He was the founder and first editor of *The Tulane Drama Review* and is the author of *The Theatre in Search of a Fix.*

HERBERT BLAU was cofounder of the San Francisco Actors' Workshop and more recently the codirector of the Repertory Theatre of Lincoln Center in New York. Author of *The Impossible Theatre* and numerous other articles on the arts, he is currently Academic Vice President and Dean of the Theatre School at the California Institute of the Arts.

HAROLD CLURMAN is drama critic of *The Nation* and author of numerous books on the theatre, including *The Fervent Years, Lies Like Truth,* and *The Naked Image.* He was executive consultant of the Repertory Theatre of Lincoln Center, where he directed the premiere of *Incident at Vichy.* A founder of the famous Group Theatre, Mr. Clurman has directed plays all over the world.

TOM F. DRIVER is Professor of Theology and Literature at Union Theological Seminary. The author of *The Sense of History in Greek and Shakespearean Drama* and numerous articles on the theatre, he has just completed a *History of the Modern Drama,* which is to be published by Delacorte.

ERIC MOTTRAM is Lecturer in American Literature in the Institute of United States Studies, King's College, University of London. He was visiting professor at New York University in 1966 on a grant from The Association of American Learned Societies.

BRIAN PARKER is Professor of English at Trinity College, University of Toronto, and is Director of the Institute for Advanced Theatre Study.

M. W. STEINBERG is Professor of English at the University of British Columbia, Vancouver, Canada.

The late ROBERT WARSHOW (1917–1955) was one of the most perceptive critics of American cultural life of our century. At the time of his death, he was an editor of *Commentary* and was rapidly becoming one of the nation's most distinguished film critics.

GERALD WEALES is Professor of English at the University of Pennsylvania. The editor of the *Arthur Miller: Death of a Salesman* volume in the Viking Critical Library, he has also written and edited numerous other books, including *American Drama Since World War II, Modern British Drama,* and *The Play and Its Parts.* He was awarded the George Jean Nathan Prize for Dramatic Criticism in 1965.

RAYMOND WILLIAMS is a lecturer at Cambridge University. He is the author of numerous books and articles on the drama, including *The Drama from Ibsen to Eliot* and *Modern Tragedy.*

Selected Bibliography

Plays (date in parentheses is of the first production)

The Pussycat and the Expert Plumber Who Was a Man, in *One Hundred Non-Royalty Radio Plays,* ed. William Kozlenko. New York, 1941.

William Ireland's Confession, in *One Hundred Non-Royalty Radio Plays.* New York, 1941.

That They May Win (1943), in *The Best One-Act Plays of 1944,* ed. Margaret Mayorga. New York, 1945.

The Man Who Had All the Luck (1944), in *Cross-Section,* ed. Edwin Seaver. New York, 1944.

Grandpa and the Statue, in *Radio Drama in Action,* ed. Erik Barnouw. New York, 1945.

The Story of Gus, in *Radio's Best Plays,* ed. Joseph Liss. New York, 1947.

All My Sons (1947), in *Collected Plays.* New York, 1957.

Death of a Salesman (1949), New York, 1949.

An Enemy of the People (1950), New York, 1951.

The Crucible (1953), in *Collected Plays.*

A Memory of Two Mondays (1955), in *Collected Plays.*

A View from the Bridge (1955), New York, 1955.

A View from the Bridge (1956), revised version; in *Collected Plays.*

The Misfits (1960), New York, 1961.

After the Fall (1964), New York, 1964.

Incident at Vichy (1964), New York, 1965.

The Price (1968), New York, 1968.

Articles and Interviews on the Theatre

"Arthur Miller on 'The Nature of Tragedy,'" *The New York Herald Tribune,* March 27, 1949, V, pp. 1, 2.

"The American Theater," *Holiday,* XVII (January, 1953).

"On Social Plays," Preface to *A View from the Bridge,* New York, 1955.

"The Family in Modern Drama," *The Atlantic Monthly,* CXCVII (April, 1956), 35–41.

"The Shadow of the Gods," *Harper's,* CCXVII (August, 1958), 35–43.

"The Playwright and the Atomic World," *Tulane Drama Review,* V (June, 1961), 3–20.

"Lincoln Repertory Theatre—Challenge and Hope," *The New York Times,* January 19, 1964, II, pp. 1, 3.

"Our Guilt for the World's Evil," *The New York Times Magazine,* January 3, 1965, pp. 10–11, 48.

"Death of a Salesman: A Symposium," *Tulane Drama Review,* II (May, 1958), 63–69.

Gelb, Phillip, "Morality and Modern Drama," *Educational Theatre Journal,* X (October, 1958), 190–202.

Allsop, Kenneth, "A Conversation with Arthur Miller," *Encounter,* XIII (July, 1959), 58–60.

Brandon, Henry, "The State of the Theatre: A Conversation with Arthur Miller," *Harper's,* CCXXI (November, 1960), 63–69.

Gelb, Barbara, "Question: 'Am I My Brother's Keeper?'" *The New York Times,* November 29, 1964, II, pp. 1, 3.

Gruen, Joseph, "Portrait of the Playwright at Fifty," *New York,* October 24, 1965, pp. 12–13.

Carlisle, Olga, and Rose Styron, "The Art of the Theatre II: Arthur Miller, an Interview," *Paris Review,* X (Summer, 1966), 61–98.

Works on Arthur Miller

Adler, Henry. "To Hell With Society," *Tulane Drama Review,* IV, 4 (May, 1960).

Bentley, Eric. *The Dramatic Event.* Boston, 1954.

Bentley, Eric. *What Is Theatre?* Boston, 1956.

Bermel, Albert. "Right, Wrong and Mr. Miller," *The New York Times,* April 14, 1968, II, pp. 1 and 7.

Bettina, Sister M., SSND, "Willy Loman's Brother Ben: Tragic Insight in *Death of a Salesman,*" *Modern Drama,* IV (February, 1962).

Brustein, Robert. *Seasons of Discontent.* New York, 1965.

Clurman, Harold. "Arthur Miller: Theme and Variations," *Theatre, The Annual of the Repertory Theater of Lincoln Center,* ed. Barry Hyams. New York, 1964.

Clurman, Harold. *Lies Like Truth.* New York, 1958.

Dillingham, William B. "Arthur Miller and the Loss of Consciousness," *Emory University Quarterly,* XVI (Spring, 1960), 40–50.

Eissenstat, Martha Turnquist. "Arthur Miller: A Bibliography," *Modern Drama,* V (May, 1962).

Findlater, Richard. "No Time for Tragedy?" *Twentieth Century,* CLXI (January, 1957).

Ganz, Arthur. "The Silence of Arthur Miller," *Drama Survey,* III, ii (October, 1963).

Ganz, Arthur. "Arthur Miller: After the Silence," *Drama Survey,* III (1964).

Gardner, R. H. *The Splintered Stage.* New York, 1965.

Goode, James. *The Story of The Misfits.* Indianapolis: Bobbs-Merrill, 1963.

Gould, Jean. *Modern American Playwrights.* New York, 1966.

Hayes, Richard. "I Want My Catharsis," *Commonweal,* LXIII (November 4, 1955).

Hogan, Robert. *Arthur Miller.* Minneapolis: University of Minnesota Press, 1964.

Huftel, Sheila. *Arthur Miller: The Burning Glass,* New York, 1965.

Hunt, Albert. "Realism and Intelligence: Some Notes on Arthur Miller," *Encore,* VII, London (May-June, 1960).

Kitchin, Laurence. *Mid-Century Drama.* London, 1960.

Lerner, Max. *Actions and Passions.* New York, 1949.

McAnany, Emile G., S.J. "The Tragic Commitment: Some Notes on Arthur Miller," *Modern Drama,* V (1962).

Meyer, Nancy and Richard. *"After the Fall:* A View from the Director's Notebook," *Theatre, The Annual of the Repertory Theater of Lincoln Center,* II, New York, 1965.

Moss, Leonard. "Arthur Miller and the Common Man's Language," *Modern Drama,* VII (1964).

Popkin, Henry. "Arthur Miller: The Strange Encounter," *Sewanee Review,* LXVIII (Winter, 1960).

Rahv, Phillip. *The Myth and the Powerhouse.* New York, 1965.

Schneider, Daniel E., M.D. "A Study of Two Plays by Arthur Miller," *The Psychoanalyst and the Artist* by Daniel E. Schneider, M.D. New York, 1950.

Seagar, Allan. "The Creative Agony of Arthur Miller," *Esquire,* LII (October, 1959).

Tynan, Kenneth. *Curtains.* New York, 1961.

Weales, Gerald. *American Drama Since World War II.* New York, 1962.

Welland, Dennis. *Arthur Miller.* New York, 1961.

Wells, Arvin R. "The Living and the Dead in *All My Sons,*" *Modern Drama,* VII (May, 1964).

Wiegand, William. "Arthur Miller and the Man Who Knows," *Western Review,* XXI (1957).

Yorks, Samuel A. "Joe Keller and His Sons," *Western Humanities Review,* XIII (Autumn, 1959), 401–7.

TWENTIETH CENTURY VIEWS

American Authors

TWENTIETH CENTURY VIEWS

British Authors

JANE AUSTEN, edited by Ian Watt (S-TC-26)
THE BEOWULF POET, edited by Donald K. Fry (S-TC-82)
BLAKE, edited by Northrop Frye (S-TC-58)
BYRON, edited by Paul West (S-TC-31)
COLERIDGE, edited by Kathleen Coburn (S-TC-70)
CONRAD, edited by Marvin Mudrich (S-TC-53)
DICKENS, edited by Martin Price (S-TC-72)
JOHN DONNE, edited by Helen Gardner (S-TC-19)
DRYDEN, edited by Bernard N. Schilling (S-TC-32)
T. S. ELIOT, edited by Hugh Kenner (S-TC-2)
FIELDING, edited by Ronald Paulson (S-TC-9)
FORSTER, edited by Malcolm Bradbury (S-TC-59)
HARDY, edited by Albert Guérard (S-TC-25)
HOPKINS, edited by Geoffrey H. Hartman (S-TC-57)
A. E. HOUSMAN, edited by Christopher Ricks (S-TC-83)
SAMUEL JOHNSON, edited by Donald J. Greene (S-TC-48)
BEN JONSON, edited by Jonas A. Barish (S-TC-22)
KEATS, edited by Walter Jackson Bate (S-TC-43)
D. H. LAWRENCE, edited by Mark Spilka (S-TC-24)
MARLOWE, edited by Clifford Leech (S-TC-44)
ANDREW MARVELL, edited by George deF. Lord (S-TC-81)
MILTON, edited by Louis L. Martz (S-TC-60)
MODERN BRITISH DRAMATISTS, edited by John Russell Brown (S-TC-74)
RESTORATION DRAMATISTS, edited by Earl Miner (S-TC-64)
SHAKESPEARE: THE COMEDIES, edited by Kenneth Muir (S-TC-47)
SHAKESPEARE: THE HISTORIES, edited by Eugene M. Waith (S-TC-45)
SHAKESPEARE: THE TRAGEDIES, edited by Alfred Harbage (S-TC-40)
G. B. SHAW, edited by R. J. Kaufmann (S-TC-50)
SHELLEY, edited by George M. Ridenour (S-TC-49)
SPENSER, edited by Harry Berger, Jr. (S-TC-80)
LAURENCE STERNE, edited by John Traugott (S-TC-77)
SWIFT, edited by Ernest Tuveson (S-TC-35)
THACKERAY, edited by Alexander Welsh (S-TC-75)
DYLAN THOMAS, edited by Charles B. Cox (S-TC-56)
YEATS, edited by John Unterecker (S-TC-23)

TWENTIETH CENTURY VIEWS

European Authors